PRAISE FOR ÊTRE

"Breaking down big ideas like entrepreneurship, financial confidence, and mentorship for the younger set at an early and important age, this book springboards today's girls to become tomorrow's moguls!"

—**Tiffany Pham**, founder and CEO of Mogul and bestselling author of *You Are a Mogul* and *Girl Mogul*

"At Ellevate Network, we believe that giving ambitious women more opportunity will make the world a better, more equal place for everyone. Our community of women role models is setting the stage for a future where girls see themselves as leaders, with the power to change things in a big way. Être girls are the next generation of changemakers, leaders, and role models that our community needs. We're proud to be building a world together where women's power is embraced and celebrated."

—**Ellevate Network**, a global community of professional women committed to helping each other succeed

"Être brilliantly does what no other organization or book does. It reaches middle school girls exactly where they are and helps them soar. Using fresh, engaging language, Être provides th___ ____ ___ ___ _____ 'entify, preserve, and foster their most auth___ ___ ___ ___ ten gets lost in the societal pressures of mid___ ___ ___ ur-ages them to become the best version o_ ___ ___ d for every middle school girl and everyor___

—**Marie Benedict**, *New York Times* bestselling author of *The Only Woman in the Room*, *Carnegie's Maid*, and *The Other Einstein*

"Middle school girls are a growing and mighty force for change. Être lays down a great road map for girls to help discover themselves and the leaders they can become in their own lives, communities, companies, and countries."

ÊTRE

GIRLS, WHO DO YOU WANT TO BE?

ÊTRE

GIRLS, WHO DO YOU WANT TO BE?

WISE WORDS FOR WORLD-CHANGING GIRLS

ILLANA RAIA
FOUNDER, ÊTRE

ÊTRE
PRESS

Published by Être Press, New York
www.etregirls.com

Edited and designed by Girl Friday Productions
www.girlfridayproductions.com

Cover & interior design: Rachel Marek
Editorial: Alexander Rigby, Laura Lee Mattingly, Erin Cusack

ISBN: 978-1-7332457-0-8

TO THE GIRLS

CONTENTS

How This Book Came To Be

Hey there, great to meet you. Seriously glad you're here. My name is Illana and I'm the founder of Être—a resource and mentorship platform for girls your age.

I feel like we're friends already.

I am also a lawyer and a lecturer, but right now I'm here for *you*: the curious, motivated, whip-smart, and often underestimated middle school girl. I'm here because I know how much you're capable of.

Why? Glad you asked.

When my daughter was in middle school and I was working at a law firm, I realized she really didn't know what my job entailed. Nor did she know what any of my working friends did. Never mind that they were surgeons and CEOs, airline pilots and news anchors; to her they were simply my friends from book club or so-and-so's mom. They were awesome and she wasn't seeing it.

This is ridiculous, I thought, *and easy to fix.*

I had been blessed with tremendous female mentors throughout my career, so why not find some for her? Why not take her to meet accomplished women with cool jobs and let her ask a zillion questions? We did exactly that, and as we bounced from office to office, I remember thinking, *Every girl should be doing this.*

Years later when I retired from law-firm life, the mentorship idea was still there.

Grateful for every role model in my past and looking for a way to pay it forward, I decided to hold a one-day girls' summit.

"I'll bring middle school girls and mentors together," I excitedly told a friend, *"and it'll be amazing!"*

"Sure, but you're kind of an idiot," she replied calmly. *"This is bigger than one day. This is a website."* And, girls, that's why it's great to have smart friends.

Because that was the day Être was born.

Wait, so what is Être? Huddle up.

Yep, mentors.

These are people who have been doing the stuff you love for a really long time and are great at it. People who can recognize a spark of something in you—a passion, a talent, an idea—and help you develop it into something impactful. Women who remember what it feels like to be a middle school girl and want to springboard you into greatness, starting now.

I'm one of these women. I know you aren't just waiting to be something when you grow up. **I think you are your most authentic self**

Être means "to be."

For one, the word is French. *Être* means "to be." I love this word and all the possibilities it evokes. I chose this word for the website I built and now for this book because it echoes my absolute favorite question to ask anyone: **Who do you want to be?**

Now, people probably ask you all the time *what* you want to be, and they mean when you grow up. But in doing this, they overlook the most important thing about you—*hello*—that you have already become someone spectacular! At exactly this moment you have abilities and interests getting ready to launch. *You are already becoming who you want to be. All you need are the right resources and mentors to help along your journey.*

right now, and I want to help you stay true to that girl. I want you to hold fast to the activities you love, stick with the sports that resonate, and raise your hand in every class. I want you to be amazing and lots of other women do too.

That's where this book comes in.

Être is a compilation of articles I've written specifically with *you* in mind. In recent years I've spent a lot of time thinking about you and your friends—breaking down big topics of the day in a format and language that are meant for you. Now I'm bringing all of this together in a handbook to make sure that you are never again underestimated and, most important, that you stay true to who you are.

We cover big topics—because I know you can handle them. **Financial confidence. Philanthropy. Innovation and entrepreneurship.** Seriously, why do some people think that it's rude when girls talk about money? It's not impolite, *it's essential*. And why do others think you are too young to make a real philanthropic difference, start your own company, or bring a clever new product to market? *News flash—they're wrong.*

The bottom line is this: *You are not too young. You are exactly the right age.* All you need are the right tools and teachers. You're holding a bunch right here.

The book is organized into ten different topics to help you become your best and most authentic self. Your new top 10 list. The first chapter, #BeSmart, celebrates your braininess, checks out STEM resources, and urges you to raise your hand, because that's everything. #BeInnovative spotlights girls

your age who are disrupting different sectors and encourages you to think outside the box. #BeWi$e opens your world to financial literacy because, despite what people tell you, you're not too young to learn about money. #BeConnected breaks down mentorship,

You are already becoming who you want to be. All you need are the right resources and mentors to help along your journey.

explaining how to find a mentor, ask for guidance, and then become a mentor yourself *(stop laughing, you are absolutely old enough to mentor a younger girl!)*, and #BeStrong amplifies athlete role models while begging you to stay in your cleats. #BeInformed explains why it's important to watch and read all the news before making up your own mind, why today's girls will be on tomorrow's ballots, and how to get ready to vote—and run. You'll learn how to use your social media prowess for good in #BeCharitable, how to cultivate courage in #BeBrave, and how to find contests to enter and ways to pursue your passions in #BeHappy. Finally, you'll walk away with a rockstar list of books to keep all of this going in #BeWellRead.

In addition to the articles and resource lists, each of these chapters includes wise words from accomplished women and inspi-

You are not too young. You are exactly the right age.

rational teens who can serve as your mentors as you read, as well as insights from girls your age across the country.

And by the way, these aren't just quotes taken from some famous people pretending to relate to girls. These are quotes given directly to Être *for* you. Answering questions submitted *by* you and girls like you. Women and girls who responded to our emails, sat for our interviews, and didn't back away when we walked right up to them on the street. In fact, they stepped forward—because they want to impact your future.

They are talking to you. They know that there is power in a pipeline and value in shared voices. And they believe, like I do, that it is not too early to talk to girls like you about *big ideas.*

It's time.

It's exactly the right time.

So dive in. Start with the chapter that appeals most to you and jump around, magazine-style. There are notes and links for when you want to learn more, and hashtags for everything you want to share later. Treat it like a coffee-table book—never mind if you don't drink coffee or even own a table. It's something to keep on hand to flip through when you need a burst of insight, fresh ideas, or a motivating pat on the back.

This book is here to help you realize more fully all the things you already *are* and to open your eyes to everything else you can

be. It's a consolidation of the Être platform, packed with tons of role models, actionable tips, and a steadfast refusal to underestimate you. So, girls, back to my favorite question: **Who exactly do you want to be?**

Let's find out together.

XO,
Illana

CHAPTER ONE
#BeSmart

You're smart. Yep, secret's out. We know there are classes you love, science fairs you look forward to all year, and debates you dominate. Science, tech, engineering, and math? You're owning them—or at least eyeing them.

Embarrassed? Don't be. The smart girl wins. For real. She gets her questions answered because she's smart enough to ask them. She gets her point across because she knows enough to voice it. These skills will serve her well throughout school, college, and her career.

Scary? Maybe a little, but stay with us.

In this chapter you'll discover why nerdy girls are cool girls, how to engineer your future, and what other award-winning smart girls out there want you to know. Think of this as a friendly text before the test, reminding you to gather your courage, unleash your curiosity, and *be* the smart girl.

> ## "Girls should never be afraid to be smart, because smart is the new cool."
>
> *—Gabriella W., Être Board member, age thirteen*

"I HATED RAISING MY HAND UNTIL I REALIZED I COULDN'T REACH AS HIGH ANY OTHER WAY."

—ÊTRE

Raise Your Hand Instead of Lowering Your Standards

Calling all middle school girls: This is for you. The following words are meant for **your ears only**. As you dive into school this year, accomplished women everywhere beg you: Raise. Your. Hand.

But I'll drop my phone.
I hate raising my hand in class.
I'll just email the teacher afterward.
I have nothing to say.

Other girls might give these excuses. Girls who are freaked out by speaking aloud, afraid of looking nerdy, or scared of just how high they can reach—they might whisper these words. But you are not those girls. You—the inquisitive and intuitive middle school girl—you know better.

Here are five reasons why you should raise your hand:

1. Raise your hand to ASK.

Ask your questions in class. Don't wait in silent hope that someone will ask them for you. Moreover, ask for help when things seem tricky. Never be embarrassed to say you need help—flag down someone you trust with, yep, that outstretched hand and ask. Answers and assistance await, so . . . #raiseyourhandtoask.

2. Raise your hand to VOLUNTEER.

See a need around you? An imbalance or an injustice? An opportunity to step in where others won't? Raise your hand to make a difference. People tend to underestimate the impact middle schoolers can have. Prove 'em wrong. Find a cause, rally your friends, speak up, and get involved. The world needs you now more than ever, girls . . . #raiseyourhandtomakeadifference.

3. Raise your hand IN FAVOR OF what you applaud.

Cheer someone on . . . it can be anyone, from a teammate to a world leader. Don't be afraid to publicly support ideas, decisions, and people that resonate with you—listen to that inner voice and follow it. Like minds are waiting . . . #raiseyourhandtojoin.

4. Raise your hand IN PROTEST OF that which you disavow.

This works both ways—if you see or hear something that doesn't sit right with you, raise your hand to say so. Take time to gather your courage and speak your mind. Clearly, thoughtfully, and—*meaningful look*—respectfully . . . #raiseyourhandtobeheard.

5. Raise your hand to HELP THE NEXT GIRL.

You will have a lot of people mentoring you this year—teachers, coaches, or maybe that cool aunt. But you are in middle school now, and younger girls look up to *you*. As you achieve your own goals, raise your hand to lead that next girl forward. We're looking at you, role models . . . #raiseyourhandtolead.

Girls, as you head to school each morning and navigate those middle school halls, keep these words in mind. Chant them like a mantra. Make them your screen saver. Whatever works.

We do not ever lower our standards. We raise our hands.

Original version published on Huffington Post

"There are no shortcuts to success. Take the time to immerse yourself in the details of what you are doing, and heed the voice in your head telling you to ask the questions you need answered. Don't worry what others may think, as they have the same questions you do but are too timid to ask. When you are told 'No' or 'That's impossible,' prove them wrong."

—*Nancy Lieberman, mergers and acquisitions lawyer, and the youngest person ever to become partner at Skadden*

When Did You Know?

When did you know you were smart?

That you wanted answers to your thousands of questions?

And when did you first sense that not everyone thought it was cool to be smart?

We asked these questions to accomplished women the first week we launched Être. These original answers are still some of our favorites.

"I used to think I got the jobs no one else wanted, but I have come to understand they are the jobs no one else can do." —*Jane Elfers, Chief Executive Officer and President of The Children's Place*

"I knew I wanted to be an orthopedic surgeon when I realized in high school that I loved working with my hands and building/fixing things. It's the best job in the world to make people feel better and get them back to the sports and activities they love." —*Dr. Beth Shubin Stein, Orthopedic Surgeon, Sports Medicine, Hospital for Special Surgery*

"Every courtroom case I've tried, every oral argument I've judged, and every brief I've written, all started with a girl who read books late into the night and loved being the smart girl. #BeSmart and never be afraid to be a reader or a student." —*Jody Rudman, twenty-five-year lawyer, former Federal Prosecutor, who presented before the United States Supreme Court*

"Of all the pilots all around the world, only 5.5 percent are females. I started flying at fifteen years old, and twenty years later I am in love with my career as a pilot of a major international airline. The feeling every time I'm at the controls, flying more than 150 people to their destinations, is a rush that cannot be duplicated. Don't ever let anyone tell you that you cannot be anything you want to be." —*RoriAnn Shonk, First Officer, A320/A321, JetBlue Airways*

"STEM (science, technology, engineering, and math) is an important part of the future for men, women, and children. It is shaping how we think, act, and talk. We, as women, are starting to use our intense knowledge to make the future by taking classes and caring about our image. We are strong, and we are the future!"

—HADASSAH F., ÊTRE BOARD
MEMBER, AGE SEVENTEEN

Spoiler Alert: The Nerdy Girl Becomes the Cool Girl

She's so, you know, math-y.
She could be the nerdiest girl . . . EVER.
She took physics. Like, on purpose.
Violently uncool.

We're not naming names. We're not tagging photos. But, middle school girls, we see you . . . slouched in the back of math class texting each other. We see you, we know you, and some of us—*nobody in particular, so stop judging*—might have been you. But on behalf of sharp, successful women everywhere—the surgeons, the programmers, the engineers, the economists—we have a spoiler for you. We know how this story ends.

The nerdy girl becomes the cool girl. Like, in a big way.

You're seeing it already—in girl power movies like *Hidden Figures* and *Queen of Katwe*. You see it on your sister's bookshelf with titles like *The Other Einstein*, *Geek Girl Rising*, and the Girls Who Code series. You see it on TV with teen-tech shows like *Mythbusters Jr.* And most important, you've witnessed it among your peers. Missed it? Check out **Maanasa Mendu**, who was named America's top young scientist at fourteen when her renewable energy invention won the Discovery Education 3M Young Scientist Challenge. Or **Kiara Nirghin**, who at age sixteen nabbed the Google Science Fair Grand Prize by developing a safer way to fight drought.

Yeah, they were in high school at the time. Probably not sitting in #thebackrow.

But here's the thing—**these girls were once in middle school, just like you.** They went to class and hung out in study hall. Maybe they traded playlists and watched YouTube videos together. Maybe they ducked the cafeteria and lived off the leftover Halloween candy in their lockers. *Btw, nothing wrong with that.* The point is, they were regular girls. With regular friends.

It's just that when they had a question, they sought an answer.

And guess where the answers were? Yep. Up front. In STEM.

Hang on, hang *on . . . don't think of STEM classes as nerdy-girl subjects.* **Think of them as tickets that get you into the best venues and in front of the rockstar thinkers.** Think of organizations like Girls Who Code, TechGirlz, Black Girls Code, and Stemettes (to name a few) as ushers that will put you at the front of the line with a VIP badge, because they have all the tools and encouragement you need. There are tons of other amazing STEM groups out there, but you'll find them. Cool girls always know how to find each other.

Admit it—the front of the line is *so much better than slouching in the back of the classroom. That's not really in anymore. You know what is?*

Curiosity.
Discovery.
Innovation.

So look around and find a problem that needs solving. There are plenty these days. Then use that lightning-quick brain of yours to join the ranks of today's teens who are changing the world by being smart girls.

Remember, when you feel your curiosity getting the better of you, that's when you're most likely to create something that makes the world better.

Engage all the resources at your disposal: take physics, join the coding club, enter the science fair. Sharpen those pencils and brandish those calculators.

Wear your nerdiness with pride.

Because at the end of the day, girls, we promise . . . there is Simply. Nothing. Cooler.

Original version published on Huffington Post

Ê-Interview with Emily Calandrelli, a.k.a. @TheSpaceGal

Love STEM but feel like you're the only one? We hear you—lots of Être girls feel the same way. So we reached out to one of the coolest nerdy girls we know—MIT engineer and Emmy-nominated TV science host and executive producer **Emily Calandrelli** (a.k.a. @TheSpaceGal)—and asked her how she handles feeling like that. Here's what she told us:

Ê: *Sometimes middle school girls can feel weird if their friends think they are too science-y. They feel nerdy if they can't wait for the science fair or just really like math classes. Did you ever feel like this, and, if so, how would you advise girls to overcome these hesitations and become the scientists and innovators they want to be?*

EC: Find friends with similar interests! It makes life a million times easier if you can make just one friend to share your interest in science and math with! And you should never be embarrassed to love STEM—those who do are the people who will have the coolest jobs when they grow up!

Looking For a Cool
Science Contest to Enter?

Calling all science-obsessed middle school girls. What if there was a larger contest that could turn your best theory into reality? What would you need?

Um, an easy way to enter . . . like, by video or something. Check.

Grown-ups who know a lot about my topic and want to help me. Experts. Check.

A real scientist who could be my advisor, like all the time. A mentor. Check.

Girls, welcome to the 3M Young Scientist Challenge. Past winners have been as young as sixth grade—*so crazy . . . text friends . . . we'll wait*—so huddle up, because we bet you have an idea you're dying to test. And we're pretty sure you like a challenge. **And we seriously believe you could win this thing.** Or other contests like it.

Our point: contests like this exist for girls like YOU to enter! We're not saying skip your school's science fair (def go and slay that one too); we're saying that it's OK to think bigger. A county hackathon. A regional science fair. A statewide contest. Or a national challenge like this one.

New chapters in our lives often start with challenges, girls. Take them on headfirst.
Share your idea.
Solve a problem.
Change the world.

Original version published on Thrive Global

Ê-NOTE: To enter the next 3M Young Scientist Challenge, head to www.youngscientistlab.com and find out everything you need to know about important dates, rules, prizes, and judging. Did we mention the prizes?

BE THE GIRL WHO LEARNS HOW IT WORKS

"Science isn't just for men and/or geniuses—it's time to break down these misconceptions. Girls, keep doing what you're doing! Your enthusiasm for science is contagious and allows you to be new advocates for science. Openly show how excited you are about science. Surround yourself with people who share your excitement so you can sustain your enthusiasm, even during the hard times."

—Dr. Jayshree Seth, 3M Corporate Scientist and Chief Science Advocate

"YOU DON'T EVER NEED TO PLAY DUMB TO BE POPULAR. PEOPLE WANT TO BE AROUND GIRLS WHO ARE SMART, SO PLAYING DUMB IS JUST . . . DUMB."

—Kyra W., Être Board member, age sixteen

"It is important for girls to be intellectually curious and excited to learn, for them to know that their ideas are just as valid as anyone else's in the room."

—*Paige M., Être Board member, age fifteen*

"Stepping forth and sharing your talents with the world is a big part of pursuing your dreams and finding success in life. The 3M Young Scientist Challenge allows students to share their talents with the world. Winning or losing a challenge such as this will help shape your future. The next chapter of your life may be written by the brave steps you take today to put your work out there."

—*Abigail Harrison (a.k.a. @astronautabby), Young Scientist Guest Judge and CEO of The Mars Generation*

Ê-Resources for STEM-Loving Girls

Here are some of Être's favorite resources for anyone interested in STEM. And STEAM. Like 'em? Keep visiting Etregirls.com for the complete list, which we update and refresh regularly. On the site, you'll also find helpful resources for Language & Culture and History & Biography, because we know no two smart girls are exactly alike, and nobody likes just one thing!

Black Girls Code—Committed to increasing the number of women of color in the digital space by empowering girls of color ages seven to seventeen to become innovators in STEM fields, BGC wants to make you a #FutureTechBoss! Explore their site and follow @BlackGirlsCode.

DiscoverE—One of our favorite STEM resources with engineering career info, activities, and even some national contests to enter. Oh, and DiscoverE helped bring the *Dream Big* movie to life (more on that in this chapter)! Discover more and follow @discovereorg.

EngineerGirl—Highlights engineering opportunities for girls while profiling current engineering stars and offering essay contests, competitions, and student blogger options. An easy place to get your feet wet and your mind working! Follow @EngineerGirlNAE.

Girls Who Code—Teaching computer science and programming fundamentals to sixth-through-twelfth-grade girls everywhere through after-school clubs, GWC just rocks. Find one near you and don't miss their helpful videos and coolest book series. *Ê-TIP:* Flip to our book list in chapter 10 and then follow @girlswhocode.

Goldieblox—Famous for their engineering toys for girls, now check out their app that teaches coding through games! Our friends at GoldieBlox have always said, "There are a million girls out there who are engineers. They just might not know it yet." Um, they mean you. Find the app on iTunes and follow @Goldieblox.

Stemettes—For STEM girls across the pond, here's an amazing resource working throughout the UK and Ireland to inspire and support young women in STEM careers through panel events, hackathons, and mentoring opportunities. *Brilliant.* Follow @Stemettes.

TechGirlz—Offering free hands-on workshops, called TechShopz, for middle school girls interested in learning about careers in tech, these Girlz are teaching web and game development, robotics, apps, editing, circuits, and more. Follow @Techgirlz.

TryEngineering—Want to learn what engineering careers will be like in 2030, hear from industry experts, play trivia games, or enter design challenges? Here you go. Oh, and don't miss their Meet an Engineer section to see what it's like to be an engineer today. Follow @TryEngineering.

500 Women Scientists / 500 Women in Medicine—You read that right, 500 female scientists, plus a new satellite group established by a few female medical school students! Sure, they're crazy busy with school and learning how to cure diseases and stuff, but they get the importance of inclusion, diversity, and female mentorship in medicine. And we just don't think that can start early enough. Check their pulse and follow @500womensci.

"Those who say girls can't be engineers have clearly never spoken to a girl before."

—Alexa K., Être Board member, age seventeen

Ê-Interview with Smart Girl Gitanjali Rao

Gitanjali Rao won the 3M Young Scientist Challenge with her innovative app for early detection of lead in water. And . . . she was eleven. When we stopped cheering, Être sat down and asked her a few questions about the experience.

Ê: *How did you first start thinking about your project?*

GR: I was originally inspired by the Flint water crisis after being introduced to it through a STEM lab and by watching the news. **I was nine years old at that time,** and I continued to research and follow it for the next couple of years.

I then saw my parents testing for lead in water at home, and that is pretty much what sparked the idea of using technology to solve the problem.

Using test strips and sending them to labs was time consuming, inaccurate, and expensive. I really wanted to do something to change this, not just for my family but for the residents of Flint and places like it around the world.

I heard about carbon nanotube [CNT] sensors being able to detect hazardous gas in the air, so I decided to use a similar CNT-based sensor to detect lead in water. I further extended it to connect to a mobile app for displaying the results!

Ê: *How did you seek out experts and mentors? Were you nervous to ask?*

GR: I had several STEM-lab managers (4-H club, STEM Scouts, and a few more) who introduced me to the challenge and encouraged me to enter the contest.

Once I was selected as one of the finalists, I was introduced to Dr. Kathleen Shafer, a 3M scientist. She guided me in making my idea a reality.

Throughout the whole process, I reached out to experts in the materials-science and nanotechnology fields to get more information about my idea. My teachers at STEM School Highlands Ranch helped me by providing access to a safe high school lab and a 3-D printer and guiding me through creating a mobile app.

My advice for finding mentors is to create a plan of study or research in whatever field you are passionate about, and then reach out to experts or professionals in that field. **I was initially nervous about reaching out . . . but this experience made me realize that the worst answer you may get is a no. So why not try?** I always asked my mentors their expectations of a mentee and consciously made sure that I met their expectations or exceeded them!

Want to Hear More about Engineering Your Future?

We love bragging about our role models, and Être BFF **Morgan DiCarlo** is no exception. You've got to meet her. Morgan was selected as one of America's top 10 new faces of civil engineering in 2015, and her scientific work was honored by the American Society of Civil Engineers and the Disney Imagineering Innovation contest. She is a TEDx speaker, a former NASA climate researcher, and a recipient of the prestigious National Science Foundation Graduate Research Fellowship. Check out what she wants *you* to know!

On why we need girls in STEM:

"*We need to recruit more people into STEM in general. These fields drive our economy, and they make the world a better place to*

live. *Young women are a hugely untapped pool of possible recruits for engineering."*

On gender equity in civil engineering:

"*Civil engineers design the world around us—a world that all of us share. Women (fifty percent of the population) should have an equal hand in that design."*

On mentoring:

"*It is hard to be motivated to pursue something if you don't see any people you relate with. This is what inspired me to jump in as a mentor to younger students—it was important to me to show other girls that it is possible that someone just like them is having fun and studying engineering."*

We know. She rules.

STEM Movies for Smart Girls

To all the girls who love Legos and look forward to science class, whose notebooks overflow with ideas, and whose favorite words are *what if . . .*

We have found your movies. Not. Even. Kidding.

Grab some friends and your popcorn, and get ready to meet some role models on-screen.

First up, *Dream Big: Engineering Our World*. This is a soaring and breathtakingly fresh movie for any girl looking to engineer her future.

Self-described as the first giant-screen film to answer the call of the STEM initiative, *Dream Big* does more

than just inspire smart kids to become engineers. It highlights the journey of three young female engineers, holding them up as beacons to light the way for today's girls to become tomorrow's innovators.

Tomorrow's city shapers.

Tomorrow's bridge builders.

Need specifics?

Listen as **Menzer Pehlivan** tells you what it was like to experience a devastating 7.6-magnitude earthquake *at age thirteen* . . . and then watch as she shows you how twisting the facade of one of the world's tallest buildings secures it against similar force.

See *students your age* cross a chest-high river to get to school, and then cheer along with the rest of the audience as **Avery Bang** designs and implements bridges throughout developing countries to help get kids to class and connect the isolated.

Applaud wildly as **Angelica Hernandez** leads her robotics club to national victory by devising an underwater robot named Stinky who outcompetes machines from some super famous college teams. Oh yeah, *she was in high school* at the time.

THINK BIG TODAY

IMAGINE
what
YOU CAN
BUILD

Étre

Next up, *Hidden Figures*. Based on the true story of three female mathematicians who came to be known as the "human computers," this film follows the first African American women to rise through NASA's ranks during the US space race with Russia. Inspiring? Yes. Heaven for math nerds that also includes a little car karaoke? One hundred percent. History-changing story in terms of race and gender in top-tier STEM roles? You betcha.

Want more? Check out *Temple Grandin*, *Queen of Katwe*, and *Underwater Dreams*.

These movies are important because at some point in your life people may try to tell you that girls aren't made for STEM. They may not say it overtly; it might be a look, a throw-away comment, or a quiet attempt to redirect you. But you'll know that what they're saying is that science and engineering are better left to boys because they are . . . um, boys.

Oh. Come. On.

When that happens, go back to the movies. Listen to bridge-builder Avery Bang tell Être that "engineering is for the dreamers—the kids who build sand castles and forts and imagine the ship in the playground equipment. In my experience, girls are some of the *best* dreamers, and become some of the most creative engineers."

Think of earthquake warrior Menzer Pehlivan, who urges you to "believe in yourself. It doesn't matter how difficult it can be at times. Believe that you can make a change in this world and in others' lives . . . and that engineering is a fantastic way to do it! Through engineering, you can change cities and build structures that will outlast your lifetime."

But above all, listen to the little voice inside you that whispers the answer in math before it's given by the teacher.

That voice that asks, What if?

Girls, you are built for engineering.

Original version published on Huffington Post

Be Smart . . . with a Squad

The feeling is familiar. The right answer is flicking you in the forehead and the teacher is scanning the room. You might know it. Or you might not, because nothing in this class is making any sense this week. The new girl gets it, though, and as her hand goes up, your heart sinks. Your eyes narrow and you want to hate her, except . . . except why should you hate her? You sit up a little. Why hate her when you could befriend her? Study together and actually get a freaking grip on this subject? Plus, she looks nice and she doesn't know anyone. You feel a squad coming on.

There's actually a name for this idea. It's called **Shine Theory**. Coined by podcasters and BFFs **Ann Friedman** and **Aminatou Sow**,

the premise is "I don't shine if you don't shine." Flipped another way, "I succeed when I see you succeed, and I want to help you succeed."

Why do some people think this is beyond middle school girls?

Why—instead of painting middle school girls as ultracompetitive, out-for-themselves, can-only-reach-their-goals-by-trashing-someone-else *(stop, lean against locker to catch breath)*—don't people see the girls who are already striving to lift each other up?

They're right there—the ones who cheer their lungs out when a teammate scores the goal and fist-bump the incoming class president as she passes in the hall. The ones who leap up and applaud the new girl's heart-cracking choir solo and spread the word when the super shy girl wins an award.

It's especially important to be one of these girls in the classroom. Some argue that what happens in the classroom translates later in life to the boardroom. We know . . . that's a long way off, but there's truth to that theory. Here are three simple reasons why you want to be smart with a squad, starting now:

1. Power in numbers. This is just basic math (which, *ahem*, we know you're good at): five smart girls are better than one. Rather than trying to cut each other down so only one can stand out, band together in a particular subject. Harness that brainpower, leverage each other's ideas, and work as a unit. It will take only one study session to realize that together, you are unstoppable.

2. Confidence is contagious. When you throw your head back and dance like a lunatic after your friend who was divorcing algebra finally gets an A, two things happen: you support a friend who worked hard and deserves it, and you realize the *entire cafeteria is staring at you, but you don't care. At all.* Bolstering another girl's confidence has the added benefit of strengthening your own, and that's just all kinds of good.

3. **Asking elevates others.** Too often we dive into our phones and info-surf alone just so we don't have to ask anyone else for help. After all, there must be some three-minute videos that explain osmosis or what prokaryotes do. And there are. But by asking a smart classmate for help, you are allowing them to shine. And their explanation not only enlightens you, it illuminates them. *Bonus point:* You show other girls that it's OK to ask, and that it doesn't make you any less smart. Everyone wins.

The women you see changing the world today are undoubtedly leaning on each other—drawing strength and support from

their collective successes. Maybe they learned to do that during their first job, or maybe it was earlier, in college or even high school. But we bet if you asked them, they'd say they wished they had started in middle school.

So leverage your smarts. Multiply your courage. Make each other shine.

Be smart with a squad . . . and definitely dance like lunatics.

"I think it's important for girls to build each other up instead of tearing each other down — because we should be united, not divided."

—*Alyssa L., Être Board member, age sixteen*

Ê-Interview with the STEAM Squad

What is the STEAM Squad? It's a brand-new collection of some of the **top science, tech, engineering, art, and math teens** today! They met online through Twitter and Instagram and created a group to cheer each other on and encourage other kids to embrace STEAM. Être could not love this idea more, so we reached out to the squad with a ton of questions. Here are some of our favorite answers:

Ê: *If middle school girls who love STEAM subjects could put one piece of advice up in their lockers—to look at and inspire them every day—what do you think it should be?*

JSS: My advice to girls that want to be in STEAM is "even if you're the first, be proud that you are a leader." What this means is that even if you're the only girl in a program, class, or job, you are a leader because you are the first and you are showing that girls can do it and girls are interested. *—Julie Seven Sage, age fifteen, producer of 7 Sage Labs YouTube channel and the Supernova Style Science News.*

AW: Kids are not the "future"; we are here now. We are not going to change the world "someday"; we already are. *—Allie Weber, age fourteen, mythbuster on the Science Discovery Channel show* Mythbusters Jr. *and Host of the Tech-nic-Allie Speaking YouTube channel.*

TR: Wow! Lots of inspiring words could be said; my favorites are: Be YOU! You're worth it. Practice makes progress not perfect. And this quote: "Don't let anyone rob you of your imagination, your creativity, or your curiosity. It's your place in the world; it's your life. Go on and do all you can with it and make it the life you want to live." That's from my idol, Dr. Mae Jemison, the first African American woman astronaut in space. *—Taylor Richardson, age sixteen, changemaker at the first White House State of Women Summit, award-winning speaker, activist, philanthropist, and aspiring astronaut.*

IH: I have three inspiring phrases: (1) When everything seems to go against you, remember that the plane takes off against the wind. (2) If you can dream it, you can reach it, you can do it! (3) Whatever your decision is, make sure it makes you happy. *—Ivanna Hernandez, age sixteen, member of the Apollo Astronomy Group that helps children in under-served areas develop a love of STEM; interested in aerospace engineering and becoming the first Latin American woman to travel to the planet Mars.*

JR: Don't give up, believe in yourself, and failure is the key to success. *—Jordan Reeves, age fourteen, designer, disability advocate, Mattel collaborator designing Barbie dolls with prosthetic limbs, and coauthor of* Born Just Right.

#BESMART
IN TEN WORDS OR LESS:

RAISE YOUR HAND INSTEAD OF LOWERING YOUR STANDARDS.

CHAPTER TWO

#BeInnovative

Be innovative. What exactly does that mean? Does it mean you need to go out and launch the next big thing that's so amazing that SpaceX makes you an offer . . . all before gym class? Um, no. *But that would be cool.* What it means is that there are problems big and small that need solving and products that need inventing, and we think you are *just the girls to do it!* Yep . . . you. With all the resources available online these days, developing an idea and sharing it with grown-ups who can help bring it to market has never been easier.

In this chapter, we'll talk about what it means to innovate, why girls make great founders, and why you are not too young for *any of this.* To further that point, you'll meet inspiring teen founders, entrepreneurial female mentors, and a slew of targeted resources to get you started. So mute that doubting voice and believe this: That project you've been toying with . . . pursue it. Your ideas have worth. And the world is listening.

> "Be the girl who invents the product, patents the process, or creates the startup that changes the world."
>
> —*Être*

Five Reasons Why Girls Make Great Founders

A middle school girl sighs.

A brand-new school year is well under-way, so why does everything feel *exactly the same*? The after-school club lists are up. OK, sure, she'll join the same one as last year. Tryout posters hang in the halls . . . she'll audition again, as usual. Same teams, same cliques, same councils, same mix. Is she jaded at this early age? Cynical already?

She blows a yawning bubble of gum over her braces.

Nope . . . she's bored.

We get it. But here's what we'd tell her, and you: It's one thing to *join* something—a committee, a sport, a chorus—and these can

absolutely be valuable experiences. **But it's quite another to start something.** To bring something new and fresh to your school and leave the place just a little bit different when you head off to high school.

Ask any accomplished woman in a lead-ership role for her best back-to-school advice, and you'll probably get something like: **"Be a founder."**

Mmmmkay . . . what's a founder?

Great question.

Founders are innovators. Originators. People with purpose, passion, and a great idea who get there first. When you hear the word *founder*, you might think of grown-ups who built giant companies in tiny garages. With black turtlenecks. And bank accounts.

But here's the thing . . . many of the traits that define famous founders can be cultivated at an early age. *Your age.* Maybe even while wearing a hoodie. And no matter what you do next in high school, college, or beyond, **the qualities you develop by founding some-thing now could last you a lifetime.**

Yeah, I so don't have those traits.

Spoiler alert . . . you do. And to prove it, here's a list of five characteristics often shared by founders. See if any of these—*cough, pointed look*—sound like you:

1. Founders RECOGNIZE A NEED.

Is there a club or sport your school doesn't yet have? A chapter of a larger organization no one has started? Think about an issue over which like minds might connect or a problem diverse minds could solve. When you find yourself leaning against your locker saying, *"I wish our school had . . . ,"* stop. It *could* have it. It has you to make it happen.

2. Founders CREATE.

If the issue or activity resonating with you isn't being represented at your school, you've found an opportunity. A niche. That's how you know it's time to innovate and build. And, hey—it's OK to think big here. There is huge freedom in creating something entirely new where nothing existed before.

3. Founders TAKE RISKS.

Sure, starting something can be scary, but *founders are fearless!* Step out of your comfort zone and walk up to the mic at the next school assembly. Have the courage to present novel ideas to new faces and listen to their contributions in return. Then be brave enough to move the best ideas forward.

4. Founders LEAD.

And here's where it all comes together, girls: the opportunity to lead. You've matched a solution to a need and communicated it well. Now it's time to organize, rally a team, and get to work. Raise awareness on campus and on social media (where, we know, you *rule*), generate enthusiasm, and lead the way.

5. Founders LEAVE A LASTING CONTRIBUTION.

This one is icing on the cupcake—the way you pay your mentors forward and your school back. By establishing a new club, contest,

or committee, you are leaving your mark. Ensuring a legacy. Guaranteeing that your school will be different, and better, simply because you and your classmates were there. You know what that sounds like? It sounds like changing the world, little by little.

So this year, be the girl who starts something.

It's not just that colleges say they look for impactful leadership roles in future applicants. **It's that school communities grow when new ideas are planted.** And some of the best clubs out there can be started by a single kid with a great idea.

Girls who do this are the ones colleges will recruit. Employers will hire. Voters will elect.

Because girls with the courage to launch will become women with the confidence to lead.

Girls . . . look around. Step up. Be a founder.

Original version published on Huffington Post

If You Could Follow Some of Our Favorite Female Founders on Twitter Today!

Some women—well, a lot of women—were innovators before social media was even invented. Imagine if we could follow their feeds today! Meet some of history's greatest female inventors via their fictional handles, brought into the modern age just for you:

Marie Curie
@FoundtheCurie
First woman to win a Nobel Prize (for introducing the theory of radioactivity) and the first person—and only woman—to earn two Nobels! #SoNiceIWonItTwice

Beulah Louise Henry
@LadyEdison
Creator of 110 inventions (and 49 patents), including one of our favorites, a vacuum ice-cream freezer. #110Flavors

Grace Hopper
@AmazingGrace
Designed one of the first Harvard computers in 1944. It's rumored that her removal of moths from a machine sparked the phrase *debugging*. #DontBugMe

Marie Van Brittan Brown
@MarvelousMakerMarie
Nurse who invented the first home security system, laying the groundwork for push-button alarms, two-way microphones and closed-circuit TV systems. #BeAlarmed

Ada Lovelace
@AdaGirl
Her computer programming work led to the first algorithm intended to be carried out by a machine. #ShesGotAlgorithm

Sarah Goode
@GoodeIdeas
First African American woman to obtain a US patent (for a bed that converted into a desk when not in use!). #PatentlyAmazing

Hedy Lamarr
@HeadyFullOfNumbers
Famous movie star who developed a communications system used by the US military that now underlies technology like Bluetooth and Wi-Fi! #SorryItsClassified

"The idea for my company started in middle school, so my advice is when you have a new idea . . . put it to paper! Prototype it and connect with industry experts. Ask for five minutes of their time. These are all things I did in middle school."

—Tiffany Pham, founder and CEO of Mogul; bestselling author of You Are a Mogul and Girl Mogul

If You're an Entrepreneurial Girl with a Cool Startup Idea . . . Don't Give Up.

Girl practices sales pitch in bathroom mirror.

"Hi—I have an amazing idea that will solve a problem.

It will fill a need in the market, and no one has done it yet.

I need your help to make my idea a reality.

Because . . . um, you're a grown-up."

Girl sighs and stares at herself. She hates her voice. She seriously hates her bangs. But she loves her idea. Who, she wonders, would ever even listen to her?

We would. Lots of people would.

Jordan Reeves, the fourteen-year-old girl who patented her now-famous glitter-shooting prosthetic arm, would. **Shakeena Julio** and **Allieberry Pitter**, the fifteen- and sixteen-year-old engineers who developed a scooter-driven cell phone charger, would. **Mercer Henderson**, the seventeen-year-old CEO of a company designed to encourage young entrepreneurs, would. And all five of the female tech founders profiled in the new movie *She Started It* definitely would.

She Started It, described as "the first film to show the behind the scenes of running a tech startup as a young woman," follows five female entrepreneurs, some starting in their teens, from their childhood homes and college dorms to Silicon Valley hallways to fund their dreams.

How did they do it?

With grit. With pizza. With wise words from role models like GoldieBlox CEO **Debbie Sterling**, former White House CTO **Megan Smith**, and **Ruchi Sanghvi**, the first female engineer at Facebook. And lots more pizza.

They knew they had innovative ideas.

What they didn't know was whether anyone would listen.

But they plugged in their headphones and practiced their pitches. They learned new skills, sought out experts, and faced failure. And when parents and friends suggested that *maaaaaybe* it was time to give up, they didn't.

Sound like you?

These girls started out a lot like you. Their friends were some of their closest advisors; they wore flip-flops to meetings, and their briefcases were backpacks. But more than that, they were frequently underestimated because of their youth and gender.

Hmmmm . . . sound familiar? Right. So what advice would these young founders give YOU—the middle school girl with a thousand ideas?

Well, we wondered too. So we went ahead and asked *She Started It* director and producer **Nora Poggi**. Here's what she wants you to know:

The young women featured in She Started It *were not born confident and resilient, nor were they born geniuses. They practiced and worked hard at it. The best advice they can give you and what we learned from them is, everyone has the potential to create, and it is up to you not to give up, to practice your pitch, to seek out mentors, and to work hard. Don't surround yourself with naysayers. Seek out people who believe in you and who uplift you. In the words of Stacey Ferreira, who is featured in the film: "Start somewhere and start today!"*

We couldn't say it any better.

This is why you should hold fast to your creativity.

This is why you should keep your goals firmly in sight.

Yes, venture capital funding and female underrepresentation in Silicon Valley are grown-up topics. But **entrepreneurship**, developing a **tolerance for risk,** and having **a superhero work ethic**—these are ideals that you can adopt starting now.

Middle school is not too early to pursue an idea you think could make a difference. Or solve a problem. Bonus points if it's scalable and grown-ups can help you bring it to market. You get the superhero cape if it has a socially useful or philanthropic component.

To all the female founders who fought the odds and paved the way for the next gen of innovators—thank you.

And to all the girls out there with a cool startup idea: Don't. Give. Up.

The world needs new ideas.

And it's waiting for you.

Original version published on Huffington Post

"You only need one yes to have your dreams come true."

—*Sammy Wolfe, inventor and youngest entrepreneur at the 2018 Consumer Electronics Show*

"Research proves there's huge, untapped potential in young women— once in business, young women win. In fact, although college women make up just 22 percent of participants in college venture competitions, 51 percent of the winning teams have a female founder. This is just further proof that women can outperform in business, and it underscores why we need to expose girls like you earlier to business and entrepreneurship. Because whether you ultimately work for a large company trying to compete or for yourselves in the growing gig economy, these are the skills you'll need: adaptability, collaboration, and resiliency."

—Jennifer Openshaw, CEO of Girls with Impact

Ê-Interview with Teen Inventor and Author Jordan Reeves

OK, now you have to meet **Jordan Reeves**. Jordan was born with a left arm that stops just below her elbow, but that hasn't stopped her from doing anything. At age eleven—*stop, let that sink in*—with the help of a 3-D printer, **she built a glitter-shooting prosthetic and started a movement**. Her other 3-D inventions have since been featured on TV and at events like Maker Faire, TEDx, and more. She and her mom just released the book *Born Just Right* (see it in our book list at the end of chapter 10), and her foundation Born Just Right allows her to be an advocate for other kids with limb differences. Oh, and she's a CrossFit athlete. Obviously, we had questions.

Ê: *We seriously love your* Born Just Right *mission and are so excited about your new book! What made you decide to write a book, and were you nervous about becoming an author at such a young age?*

JR: I don't see a lot of disability stories in middle school chapter books. There are a lot of stories in children's picture books. That's why I worked with my mom to write something for middle schoolers. I was a little nervous about the book, and I used to get nervous about how kids at my school would react when they found out I wrote a book.

Ê: *You talk about how important STEM education is and we totally agree! How old were you when you first became interested in STEM, and what would you say to middle school girls who sometimes get discouraged from pursuing STEM subjects?*

JR: You should just give it a try. You might be surprised to see how STEAM (I like adding that *A* for arts) is a part of everything in our lives. I discovered design when I was ten, and it feels really amazing when you can make an idea become real.

Ê: *We know the design for your 3-D prosthetic arm changed a lot over time . . . are there new things you are developing or engineering right now? Do you have a favorite?*

JR: I'm still working on my glitter blaster because the glitter spills sometimes when I'm not shooting it and there's still some glitter in the arm. I'm also working on an arm that's kind of like a Swiss Army Knife, but it is voice-controlled and can deliver tools I need when I'm designing, like a scraper to get things out of my 3-D printer, pens, pencils, and scissors. My favorite thing I'm doing right now is renovating my bedroom!

"GIRLS CAN MAKE A DIFFERENCE AT ANY AGE. DON'T BE DISCOURAGED IF YOU ARE TOLD YOU ARE TOO YOUNG."

—CAMERON S., ÊTRE BOARD MEMBER, AGE ELEVEN

Ê-Interview with Sports Innovator Sammy Wolfe

Next, say hi to **Sammy Wolfe**, who developed a revolutionary heated lacrosse stick (it heats to 100 degrees and, *in a genius move,* charges just like a cell phone) **when she was in middle school!** Now in college, Sammy is refining her product and potentially changing the game for devoted LAX athletes everywhere. Keep reading and get inspired!

Ê: *We heard you came up with the* FingerFire *idea at age eleven. How did it start, and were you worried that no one would listen because you were so young?*

SW: The idea of *FingerFire* came to me when my hands would be freezing and numb

while I was playing lacrosse. I noticed I was not able to play to my full potential with my hands not gripping the shaft of the stick correctly. This led me to walk off the field complaining to my parents about my frigid hands (like most kids do). I brought up the idea of a heated lacrosse stick to my parents, but at first, they pushed away the idea. I was relentless in showing them my passion and determination in bringing this idea to fruition. Finally, my dad agreed to be my partner and that is how the three-and-a-half-year and not-over-yet journey began.

Ê: *Lots of girls think about quitting their sport after middle school—what kept you confident and secure on the field, and what would you say to girls today to keep them playing?*

SW: You should always follow your passion. Always persevere in moments of frustration because in the end you will become a more confident and determined player.

Ê: *You've been so busy—what's happening with* FingerFire *right now?*

SW: *FingerFire Technology* has gone through many positive and exciting changes. The two Division I women's teams who tested the 1.0 prototype heated lacrosse sticks back in 2017 provided extremely positive and constructive feedback. In turn, we made changes and launched the 2.0 prototype, which included cranking up the heat to 90–100 degrees, with the same weight and still lasting the duration of a game. In addition to these two teams, we now have two other top Division I women's teams. I can't reveal the names yet but [they're] very top teams.

How to Be a Founder . . . at School!

Start something new. Build something cool. Yes . . . you.

One way to found something—leaving a place a little different and better than you found it—is to start something at your school! Maybe it's a new intramural team, art program, or a cappella group. Maybe your idea augments and refreshes an existing club—for instance, helping the finance club add a cryptocurrency group, or the debate club launch online competitions with peer schools across the globe! Think big . . . and then *start small*. A school community is the perfect place to test out your founder skills. Here are five quick suggestions for sparking change at school:

1. Look for what's missing.

Check other school websites and see if they offer after-school programs or clubs your school lacks. Now envision them at your school. Would they be a good fit? Would they generate interest? Poll other students and put a star next to any ideas that resonate.

2. Look for what's required.

What would you need in order to get these activities approved? A faculty member or coach? Practice space? Equipment? Make a list.

Ê: *If a middle school girl has a cool idea for a new invention, what would you tell her? What can girls do to pursue innovative ideas at an early age?*

SW: One thing to always remember is to never stop believing in yourself. Even if you are a young woman, your ideas *do* matter. I have received many rejections throughout this (not-over-yet) journey, but that has never stopped me. You only need one yes to have your dreams come true. If you have an innovative idea you want to pursue, share the idea with friends and family to get feedback and suggestions. For example, the way I found the product-development company I have been using (*Enventys Partners* in Charlotte, North Carolina) was by talking to a family friend that happened to know someone at that company. Connections are everything in life, so make sure to share your ideas with others because you never know what might come out of the conversation.

3. Look for helpers.

Maybe a varsity coach isn't available, but what about getting help from retired coaches or local collegiate athletes? Could a mom who works on Wall Street or in media pitch in with the finance or film club? Think outside the box for adults who can help get your idea off the ground. Gather their contact info.

4. Look for the larger benefit.

How could this new school activity benefit your greater community? A good argument for embedding your new idea in your school is to highlight its potential for larger impact. If your idea involves philanthropy or mentorship, for example, how could you engage students at your school to help your neighborhood, town, or county? Any club that can reach beyond your school grounds with a positive message has a greater chance of being endorsed. Plus, you'll be making a bigger impact with your small step! Win-win.

5. Look for approval.

Pick one or two school administrators who you think will be receptive to your idea, and present the research you've done. Walk them through steps 1 through 4 in a clear, thoughtful way and answer their questions with candor. If they ask something you don't know, write down the question and promise to find out. Make an appointment to come back with the answers and any additional material they need. See if they would like to directly contact any of the adults you have mentioned as your helpers. Set a deadline for a decision.

Think of this as your first founder's pitch. You don't know how it will turn out, and school boards, like corporate boards, are budget-driven and can be unpredictable. Still, **a good idea that fills a need is worth raising and an invested student will, if well prepared, be heard.**

Think big, start small, and be heard. Your first launch awaits.

"Education is the heart of the world. Without education, our only option is to follow after family or friends. If you are educated, then you have the possibility of forming your own thoughts and opinions. Mental freedom is the best feeling there is."

—*Eden O., Être Board member, age seventeen*

From the Mind of an #InnovativeGirl

"Être means 'to be,' and it helps young girls discover who they want to be. I'm passionate about this—no girl should feel discouraged from doing what she loves. I was so engaged by the group that the summer after sophomore year in high school, I reached out to the organization with an idea:

Could I bring Être to my school and invite local guest speakers to act as mentors?

From that one idea, Club Être was born and set in motion.

I approached the administration at my school and explained the idea. I answered every question and researched what I didn't know. When the club was finally approved, over fifty middle school girls signed up. Since then, I haven't looked back. During meetings, middle schoolers ask the speakers whatever they want, and then I conduct additional interviews that get posted online. I ask questions I think girls deeply care about: how to navigate intersectional politics or, more practically, how to balance school/work with a personal life. It brings me joy to see all of these girls excited by female empowerment and how together we might achieve it.

Just as meaningful to me is that the idea itself has caught on. Since the founder posted about my club, ten Club Être chapters have been started across the US and Canada. While each of these clubs has its own story and its own heroes, I am proud that my original idea helped launch a new chapter of this great organization."

—*Samantha B.*, *Être Board member, age seventeen*

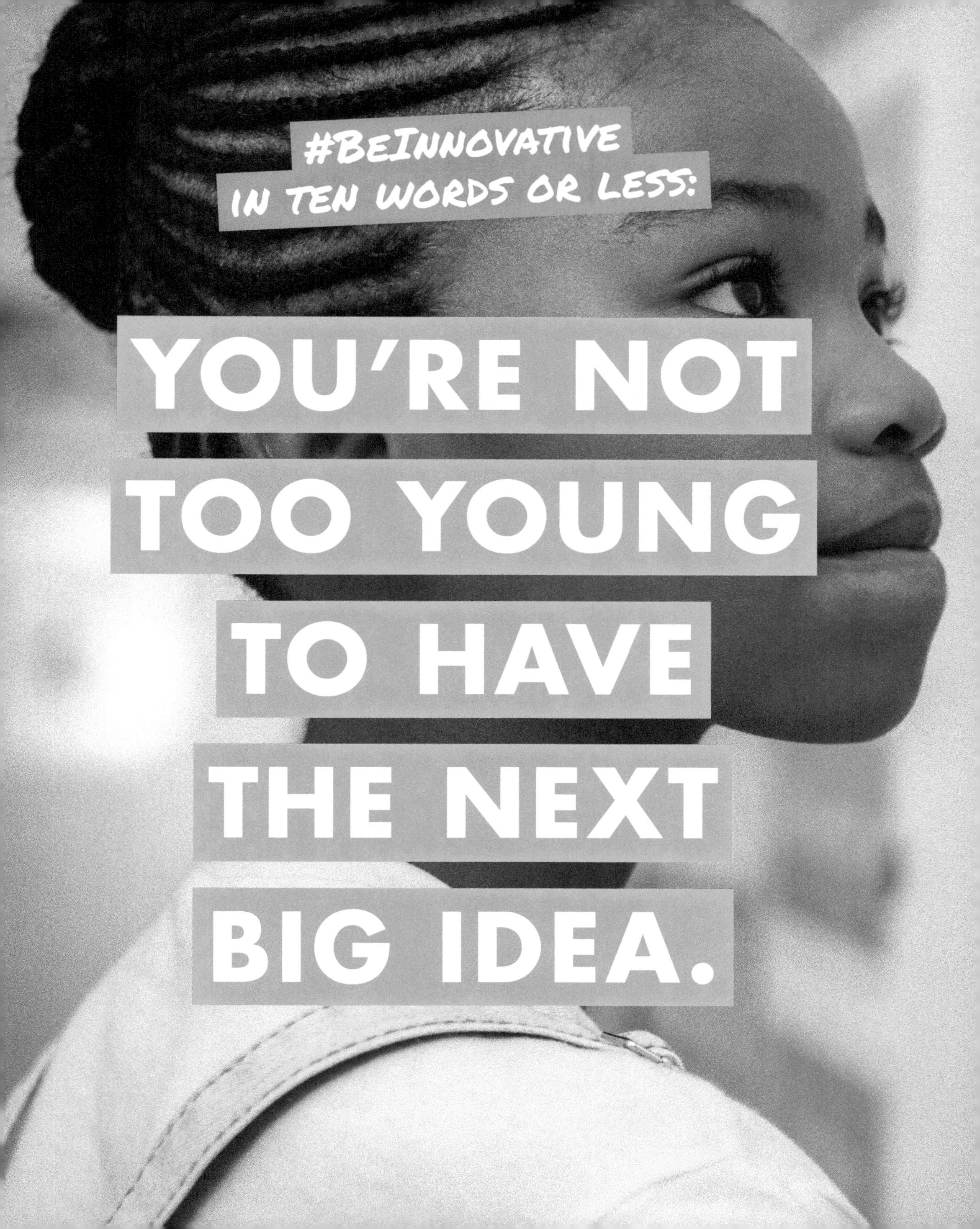
#BeInnovative
in ten words or less:
YOU'RE NOT
TOO YOUNG
TO HAVE
THE NEXT
BIG IDEA.

CHAPTER THREE

#BeWi$e

t's time. Get over it. We're gonna talk about money, girls.

Getting comfortable talking about money doesn't happen overnight. Asking questions about finance, debt, savings, and salaries can be awkward at best and down-right intimidating at worst. And that's if you're an adult! Plus, money is an area where middle school girls can be more underestimated than in most other areas. Yet you are fully capable of getting a job, saving what you make, and deciding what to do with those earnings.

So why shouldn't you be informed? Not just informed . . . wi$e. We don't want to placate you with quick answers about this. Nope—we want to help you learn from top financial institutions, helpful resources, and savvy business women.

> "Understanding the basics about earning, saving, and someday investing your money will put you light-years ahead of the crowd . . . and dependent on no one. You want to be that girl."
>
> —Être

This kind of well-rounded knowledge lays a foundation for the rest of your life. You won't flinch when someone mentions interest rates or your 401(k). You won't blush when someone tells you not to worry because they've got the finances covered. You'll look them steadily in the eye and tell them to uncover it. You'll ask your questions. You'll use your resources. **You'll handle your business. You won't depend on others to do it for you.**

And it all starts right here.

Money Talk

Ugh, you figure out the tip . . . I'm the worst at that.

I have no idea where my allowance went. Like, no idea.

My mom says it's rude to talk about money.

Math hates me, and the feeling is mutual.

Middle school girls, you have said these things. We've heard you. Heads bent together in a diner booth as you slide the check back and forth. Bewildered by the fact that you had ten dollars in your pocket *six minutes ago . . .* so where . . . did it . . . go? Chastised for asking how buying a car works. Silent in class during the money math chapter.

We get it—these topics can be intimidating, especially at first. But you know what? You're in middle school now and developing confidence in tons of new areas: trying out for higher-level sports teams, running for student council, even—*ahem*—raising your hand in class more often (hey there, chapter 1!). Don't kid yourself: you're getting braver by the minute. So why does the topic of money management send you under your desk wishing for a fire drill?

We have a theory.

While encouraging girls in STEM is getting more and more popular, it feels like less attention is being given to improving girls' financial literacy. *Pause to bang forehead slowly on desk.* Why? Not enough personal finance classes being offered to teens? Sure, that's part of it. But there is also a societal undercurrent of #badmanners related to these conversations that cannot be ignored.

When it comes to money talk, old customs seem to rear their pretty little heads. Frank discussions about finances with daughters are too often discouraged. You might get an allowance for chores performed at home, but likely no one is telling you what portion you should be saving. Or how interest works. Or how with your savings you could someday buy a share of stock in a really cool company. No one is offering information or answering your questions, because they think girls who talk about money are impolite.

Well, guess what?

That kind of talk is not impolite. In fact, it's essential.

It's essential that you learn how to earn and save money. It's equally important to understand the differences between needs and wants, between value and cost. Do you *need* the red-and-green light-up sneakers that play Christmas carols? *Skeptical eyebrow raise.* And even if you swear you do, what are the odds they won't be on sale really, *really* soon? These are the kinds of choices you'll be making for *your whole life.* So why not wise up now?

Market forces aren't mysteries, girls. They're fairly straightforward concepts that, once understood at the basic level, will make you a better decision-maker in every aspect of your life. And trust us when we tell you that **you want to be the girl who is financially confident . . . because she's the one who grows up to be independent.** She's the girl who always knows exactly what's in her bank account (because she put it there), understands how to invest her money wisely, and looks for opportunities to pay it forward.

And middle school is the perfect time to become financially informed.

When you're ready, you may even want to put your newfound knowledge to work. An allowance is one thing, but imagine having a job where you can earn your own money. Talk to your parents about it. Are there trusted neighbors looking to hire a responsible middle schooler for babysitting, snow shoveling, or dog walking? Having the **confidence** to seek and perform a job on your own is a crucial life skill. Managing your own money breeds independence and establishes good habits that will serve you throughout your life. Having the **financial awareness** to know how to save and invest what you earn will put you

light-years ahead of everyone else. And having the **generosity of spirit** to share a portion of your earnings with those less fortunate is, well, an awesome way to make a meaningful difference at any age.

Girls, it's time to get comfortable speaking about money.

Come out from under your desks. Ask your money questions and pursue the answers. Figure out the tip. Earn independently. And skip the light-up caroling footwear. Save your money and buy a share of your favorite sneaker company instead. We promise it's the wise-girl move.

Original version published on Huffington Post; republished on Huffington Post Brasil

Ê-Resources to Help You and Your Friends #BeWi$e

When it comes to money, maybe you don't know where to start. Maybe your parents don't talk to you about money yet, and it all feels a little weird. But now is actually a great time to start learning about financial independence, and there are plenty of resources out there to help. Here are some of Être's financial faves:

Ellevest: An investment platform designed *by* women *for* women, founded by girl-boss role model Sallie Krawcheck. You might not be investing with them yet, but check out their online magazine for great articles and videos on finance. Our favorite section and hashtag to follow? #DisruptMoney.

Girl Scouts Money Matters: Our BFFs at Girl Scouts have a great section on their website called "Money Matters," where they break down topics like allowances, budgeting, and debt into bite-size pieces. Être is proud to be a Girl Scouts external resource,

and we're giving them an extra badge for these money tips!

Rock The Street, Wall Street: Another Être BFF, Rock The Street, Wall Street is an organization dedicated to promoting financial literacy for girls your age. Follow them @girlsrockwallstreet and surf the "Newsroom" tab on their website for blog posts, articles, and videos to keep you, and your money, in the know. #RTSWS

The Frugal Feminista: Founded by Être role model Kara Stevens, the Frugal Feminista website offers articles for older readers on topics like budgeting like a boss, relieving student debt, entrepreneurship, and more.

UBS: Own Your Worth: This microsite has info for you to grow into or share with big sisters right now. With mother-daughter interviews, role model stories, and global stats, UBS wants you to #OwnYourWorth from day one.

Listen Up, Girls: Equal Pay

Word Problem: *If Jack and Jill work the same number of hours each week, and Jill makes eighty cents for every dollar Jack makes, how far into the next week must Jill work to equal Jack's earnings from the previous week? How does your answer change depending on Jill's race, age, or education? Show your work.*

Um, wait . . . what?

Exactly.

The math just doesn't make sense. If Jack and Jill do the same job under the same circumstances, why isn't Jill's work worth the whole dollar? And why are some of Jill's friends making even less? Jill and her friends are good at math. Jill and her friends are pissed.

We know.

This is called the gender pay gap—and **working women want to break it down for you.** This is what Equal Pay Day is all about. This day is traditionally observed on a Tuesday in April to mark how far into the next workweek (and into the next year) women have to work to match the earnings of male coworkers.

Not the most festive holiday . . . but super important in terms of raising awareness. **Because even though the math seems blindingly simple, the issue is complicated.** And worth understanding early.

Let's take a look.

First of all, it's true. On average, women make eighty cents for every dollar a man in the same job makes. Yes, it's OK to feel outraged about that. The crucial words here are *on average*—the numbers can vary depending on race, age, geographic location, and more, which means that the gap can actually be worse for women of color.

This handy infographic from our role models at Ellevate spells out the differences in emoji-speak, and we're feeling the forehead slaps.

Shared with Être by Ellevate Network

You don't need to be a grown-up to see the injustice here. But before you make posters on the back of your math quiz and plaster your locker, take a breath. This is a highly nuanced issue, and smart girls examine all the data. Like any math problem, there are variants that need to be considered.

Seriously, what? What could possibly justify this kind of disparity?

Well, some say **choices.** Some people assert that because women make different life choices than men (like whether to have children and whether to stay home to care for them and for how long), their pay can reflect those choices.

People also point to the **types of jobs** pursued. Some argue that because more men secure jobs in high-paying fields like technology or engineering, their earnings will necessarily exceed those of women who go into lower-paying fields, such as teaching or social work.

Finally, an **unwillingness to push for salary raises**. Some contend that women are less inclined to advocate for themselves when discussing salaries, so maybe they don't get the same increases their male counterparts get.

OK, so now Jill and her friends are standing *on* their desks and speaking passionately about gender bias, childcare penalties, and flat-out workplace discrimination.

We hear you. But there *is* **some good news.**

To start, there are some excellent rebuttals to these arguments out there—check out Money.com's "6 Excuses for the Gender Pay Gap You Can Stop Using" for a clear and accessible distillation of some smart research. Moreover, state and federal laws exist to protect women from true gender discrimination in the workplace, and new laws are being proposed to further close the gap. Also, more girls are taking STEM classes *(looking at you,*

math whizzes), and hopefully that means more women are going into higher-paying tech and engineering jobs. See, the gap just closed a bit more.

And maybe most importantly, *the world is paying attention.* Awareness around equal pay is rising in the era of #MeToo, with actresses like Ellen Pompeo and athletes like Carli Lloyd and Abby Wambach boldly speaking out on the issue.

So what can YOU do to ensure that by the time you and Jill are sitting in your offices, your paychecks look like Jack's?

Become informed. Read what the smart women at Ellevate, Ellevest, EY, Goldman Sachs, Lean In, Morgan Stanley, and UBS are saying about the issue on their websites, and follow #EqualPayDay and #GenderPayGap on social.

Stay aware. Listen closely to the news or at the dinner table when finance comes up. When you get your first job offer, research the average pay for your position and ask for that amount (or more). Find out what workers around you earn. *It's not rude . . . it's relevant.*

Pay is a complex issue. But equality is simple.

And hard work and fairness matter.

Girls, you can do *any job you put your mind to.* **It's our job to make sure the whole dollar is waiting for you when you get there.**

*Original version published on Medium;
republished at Ellevate.com*

Raising Our Hand and Asking Money Questions . . . on Twitter:

@etregirls: What can be done to overcome the perception that financial confidence in middle- or high-school-age girls is impolite?

@salliekrawcheck: I think this can be an issue not just for financial confidence, but for any kind. And not just in middle school, but beyond. The research is pretty clear that professional women have had to navigate a bunch of unwritten rules about acceptable behavior historically. I don't know that there's an easy answer, since these ideas can be part of our upbringing and can be an implicit gender expectation. In the workplace, talking about it, pointing it out, discussing it are means for making everyone aware and then potentially overcoming it. —*Sallie Krawcheck, CEO and cofounder of Ellevest*

"Women are equally as smart as men. There is no reason why men should be getting paid more in the same job than women. So why are men prioritized? This stereotypical label we have of men being the strong hero, as women are the damsel in distress, strengthens the superiority men have and minimizes the level of confidence in women. Without even realizing it, this label is implanted in the average human's brain. Men are not priority and should not be just because they have the advantage of being a man. Women are even more or just as talented, and their gender shouldn't be a reason for any inequality. #BeWi$e."

—Amber C., Être Board member, age fifteen

"So, any idea where your iPhone is from three years ago? Right, but if three years ago you bought one share of Apple stock (the company that makes that fun phone), you'd have an extra seventy-five dollars in your pocket. Just saying."

—Tracy Byrnes, UBS Financial Advisor, former Fox Business anchor/reporter

"GIRLS, DON'T EVER SAY 'I'M BAD AT MATH.' DON'T LET YOUR GIRLFRIENDS SAY IT. BECAUSE THE SECOND YOU DO, YOU ARE LETTING CULTURAL NORMS PRESSURE YOU OUT OF YOUR OWN PERSONAL MONEY-MANAGEMENT SKILLS AND A POTENTIAL CAREER IN FINANCE."

—*Maura Cunningham, founder and Executive Director, Rock The Street, Wall Street*

"Regardless of body parts and features, men and women are one and the same, they are created equal; therefore, they should have equal opportunity since they are working for the same cause."

—*Angelique M., Être Board member, age seventeen*

Jobs Middle School Girls Can Go After NOW

Financial confidence isn't just about knowing what to do with the money you earn. It's also about having the motivation to identify jobs you might like and the courage to go after them! *Ê-TIP:* Going after a job sounds scarier than it is. But this is no different from auditioning for the school play or trying out for the next-level travel team. You are putting your best foot forward and seeing whether your talents are a match for what the director, coach, or employer is looking for. *It's not a referendum on you as a person; it's just a straightforward pairing of skills and need.*

Getting a job in middle school is a great use of your time. It builds work ethic and resilience. It cultivates dependability and forces you to budget your time effectively. *Aaaand,* **nothing feels better than having money in your pocket when you're the one who put it there.** So, what kinds of jobs should you be on the lookout for? Here are three levels to help you *level up* to the working world.

LEVEL ONE: A simple way to start out in the working world is to identify chores you can do around the house. Anything from raking leaves, washing dishes, laundry duty, or helping with younger siblings might be worth some spending money. *Ê-NOTE:* If these aren't considered cash worthy in your house, don't worry! Regroup and renegotiate. Maybe you can trade them for a later bedtime or more weeknight screen time. Demonstrating your responsibility and business savvy will impress your parents and may just earn you privileges instead of pay.

LEVEL TWO: Once you've established that you can handle extra obligations alongside your homework and other activities, branch out. Look for trusted neighbors who might be in need of snow shoveling, weeding, cat sitting, or dog walking. These are all independent jobs that can work with your schedule and don't require extensive training. Discuss the idea with your parents or guardians (tell them who you would work for, how you would get there, what kind of supervision you'd have), and rehearse how you will ask for employment.

Then, go ahead and ask for the job. **Take a breath, it's easier than you think:**

1. State the job you're seeking in a confident voice.
2. Explain why you are a good choice for the job, what you will bring to the table, and how hard you will work.
3. Ask for guidance and feedback so you can continue to get better at your job over time.

LEVEL THREE: Let's say that goes well. You are now earning pocket money for chores and small neighborhood jobs, and you and your parents agree that you're ready for more responsibility. For this level, you'll likely need some extra training or prep. For example, if you plan to babysit alone, it would be a good idea to take a kids' CPR class or a Red Cross babysitting course. If you'd like to tutor younger kids in a subject you rock *(pause for fist bump),* start out by refreshing your knowledge of that subject and dig up the grade you got in that class. If you find work as a junior counselor at a

camp or sports clinic, make sure you understand the job parameters, skill level, and equipment they expect you to have.

ANOTHER Ê-TIP: The bigger the job responsibility, the more important feedback will be. It's critical to learn on the job, and to remember that everyone does this! Ask for guidance often and listen well—that's how you rise through any ranks.

FINAL THOUGHT: The job market for adults is changing fast. Jobs your parents had ten years ago might not exist when you enter the workforce, and the job you'll have at twenty might not exist yet. This means the job market for middle and high schoolers is changing fast too. There are probably lots of job opportunities out there that we haven't even mentioned. Creativity is everything, and you may discover a household chore or local job that no one has thought to do yet! #BeInnovative

Now get out there and make working women everywhere proud. The workforce is a great place to be— we're saving you seats!

Why Girls Should Care about Crypto

One example of a new job sector that didn't exist a generation ago is *cryptocurrency. Relax,* it's not that you're going to look for a job in crypto tomorrow (or maybe ever); we're mentioning it because this is a space where people may assume you have no interest, or even capacity, to understand. And we don't want you shut out of any job, industry, or conversation just because the subject is complicated.

So let's break it down.

#Cryptocurrency. #Blockchain. #Bitcoin. #Miners. Invisible, intangible money? No, you're not trapped in a video game. This is real life, and it's happening fast.

You said we were breaking this down.

Right. Cryptocurrency is a digital currency used to conduct transactions online, made secure by secret, encrypted codes that hide your personal info. Payments are made public in a big decentralized ledger called the blockchain, making the history easy to see and the data harder to hack.

Stay with us.

Part of what makes crypto so disruptive is that it doesn't depend on a middleman—like a store or a bank—to broker the transaction. Imagine trading on eBay . . . without a lot of fees or exchange of information.

Kinda cool.

Yes, and maybe extra interesting for women, since anonymity lessens the opportunity for gender discrimination and may offer new ways to close the gender gap.

So, are women all over this? Not entirely. According to Bloomberg, 71 percent of all digital currency is owned by men. And—*wait, it gets worse*—according to the *New York Times,* only 4 to 6 percent of cryptocurrency investors are women. Statistics like these are startling, and they need to change. But lucky for you, women are making some very real strides in crypto today.

"Gender disparity in crypto is dangerous," Mogul CEO **Tiffany Pham** told Être when she organized a girl-focused crypto conference, "because the early days of an industry are often when fortunes are made—and those big winners then choose whom to invest in and what to build next, launching a cascade of consequences for women."

"Blockchain is poised to change the way our economy works at a fundamental infrastructure level," added **Amanda Gutterman**, advisor and former CMO of ConsenSys. "This type of opportunity to help reform how the world works doesn't happen often in human history. The clay is still wet, so let's roll up our sleeves."

Sleeves. Rolled.

Kelsey Cole, cofounder and then-Chief Strategy Officer of Adbank, couldn't agree more, noting that "in order to truly disrupt the global financial system with crypto, we need more women participating in both the creation of cryptocurrencies and investment in them. **It's our turn to step up and bring our own seats to the table instead of waiting for men to invite us there.**"

In other words, this cryptocurrency thing is moving at the speed of light and women don't want you left behind. They want you to read, listen, and become informed.

Because when material is complicated and technology is developing quickly, early exposure to experts is crucial. **That way, you are ready when innovation like this streaks across the world. Or across your wallet.**

Crypto has the potential to reinvent the way we transact, trade, invest, vote, store medical information, and so much more. Granted, there are lots of issues still to be hashed out—how it all gets implemented, scaled, safeguarded, and regulated—and those conversations are taking place right now. Someday, you may want to join them.

It's complicated, but smart girls like you—particularly those used to video games and virtual currency—can grasp it, no sweat. And here's the real point: **it is unacceptable to be left out of something because it seems too new, too intangible, or too complicated to grasp at first blush.**

Read up. **Ask questions. Nothing is too complex for smart minds to start exploring.**

Original version published on Medium

"Financial literacy is an integral part of our lives. Regardless of the barriers that can hinder girls from pursuing careers in finance, we have the power and the grit to overcome anything. Men and women are equal. There shouldn't be any difference between a male or female manager, and individuals must receive equal treatment for the same job."

—*Bryll B., Être Board member, age seventeen*

"GIRLS NEED FINANCIAL SECURITY AND SHOULD SET GOALS RELATED TO THAT. FINANCIAL FAILURES NEED TO BE DISCUSSED TOO—NOT JUST THE SUCCESSES!"

—Asha Castleberry, US National Security expert, military veteran, professor, and public speaker

What to Do with Your Money

Heyyyyyy, now—girl with a job in the house! You are working and making some money. Your *own* money. And it *feels great.*

Feels empowering.

Feels like you can't keep it in the sneaker box under your bed forever.

So, now what? What exactly are you supposed to do with the cash you are earning?

First, any numbers that come after this sentence are just **suggestions.** Guidelines. A general sense *(we almost said cents, but spared you).* How much of your earnings you decide to save, spend, donate, or bury in the yard is up to you. That's the cool thing about having *your own money.* Only you and your parents know what your weekly needs are and where your long-term goals point. Any percentage or threshold mentioned here should be weighed against your personal and household needs so you can make your own decisions.

Second, money is **personal.** This is true in middle school and at middle age. You don't owe anyone outside your household any explanations about what you've earned or how you're spending it. As you get older, you may decide to share salary info with your coworkers in the interests of securing equal pay (flip back a few pages and read *that* word problem), but a good rule of thumb generally is that your money is your business.

OK, back to the **guidelines**. According to our very wi$e friends at Ellevest, lots of grown-ups divide their take-home pay by a 50/30/20 rule. To understand this, picture three buckets: 50 percent of their earnings go in the needs bucket (stuff they have to pay for, such as rent, bills, groceries, etc.); 30 percent goes in the wants bucket (things they don't need but still want, like vacations or a new TV); and 20 percent goes in the future bucket (toward things that impact their financial future, such as paying down debt, investing, and saving for your college education).

The buckets at your age will look different (and maybe a little more fun). Think about a very general 50/25/25 rule:

Fifty percent to spending.

You worked hard and should get to enjoy having your own spending money. Your spending doesn't necessarily need to go toward rent and

INDEPENDENCE IS EVERYTHING. START EARLY.

groceries yet (though your parents will brag about it for weeks if you offer a few dollars toward the family ice-cream budget), so the whole 50 percent can be used for day-to-day expenditures (like the snack bar at school or gas when you start driving) as well as those unexpected expenses you'd rather handle yourself (like concert tickets or repairing a cracked phone screen . . . again!).

Twenty-five percent to savings.

Here's where your long-term goals come into play. Are you saving for a summer program, a car, or college? Want to handle a few holiday gifts all on your own next year? That's what savings are for. A savings account is a place where you can leave your money alone and let it grow. You can also invest a portion of your savings—it's a nice feeling to have your money working for you. Lots of banks have savings account options for kids and other

introductory resources; the next time you stop in on family errands, ask for some info, or flip back to the websites we mentioned earlier in this chapter.

Twenty-five percent can actually go to charity!

Yep, you will be financially able to contribute a small portion of your hard-earned money to make a difference. You'll learn more about that in the #BeCharitable chapter (see chapter 7 for how to identify causes that resonate, how to verify where your money is going, and where it will have the most impact), but it's never too early to incorporate philanthropy into your financial plans.

Whether you follow a 50/25/25 rule or make up your own formula, the bucket concept is helpful and worth keeping in mind. You can do a lot of good with the money you make, from prioritizing your own expenses and relieving some household burdens to managing a savings account and giving back to those in need. The amounts might not be big, but a little goes a long way, and forming smart money habits now will turn you into a savvy investor later. And like we said, there are no hard-and-fast rules as to where your money should go. But following rough guidelines can help make you #Wi$e4Life.

#BEWI$E
IN TEN WORDS OR LESS:

FINANCIAL CONFIDENCE IN GIRLS ISN'T IMPOLITE. IT'S ESSENTIAL.

CHAPTER FOUR

#BeConnected

We know—you're already super connected. When you meet new friends and friends of friends, you immediately exchange info, follow each other on social, and regularly rain hearts and applause all over their feeds. You could teach a course in connecting.

What we're talking about here is a different kind of connection. The kind that lays a path and builds a pipeline for what's to come. The kind of connecting you're doing today is for *now*. The kind of connecting that spurs networks and mentors is for *later*.

Breathe. Not later like *I-have-a-job-and-where-is-my-briefcase-because-I-have-a-giant-networking-lunch* later. (Although this is good practice for stuff like that.) We mean later like next year in school, when you want to enter a regional science fair and need an advisor. Or when you decide you want to get better at coding or basketball and need to find an expert to help you. Or when you want to learn more about volunteering at an animal shelter or on a political campaign, but you don't know where to start. That's where mentors come in.

This chapter guides you through what mentorship looks like in middle school, how to connect with mentors—specifically female mentors—in a safe, smart way, and how you could mentor a younger girl. You'll learn about networks, paying it forward, and what future jobs might look like. Connections and mentors matter, girls—as early as middle school. And anyone who tells you otherwise doesn't have their eyes open wide enough.

Mentors Matter

Everywhere you turn, you see magazine covers telling girls that what you really need this month is a particular planner, a sparkly journal, or an app that will single-handedly make this your #BestYearYet. Now planners are great—we're planning one ourselves—but what you *really* need for a game-changing year is a mentor.

Yep, a mentor.

No, it's not a kind of breath mint. And no matter what some adults in your world might say, it's not something you're too young to have.

If you Google *mentor*, you will find zillions of long-winded explanations, mostly geared toward grown-ups in the workforce. But the concept itself is simple: Mentors are people who do what you like to do but have

been doing it longer, are super good at it, and are willing to share their knowledge with you.

Mentors serve as real-life role models, **cultivating talents** you didn't know you had, **identifying jobs** you never knew existed, and **highlighting pathways** to achieving your goals.

Nice. Sounds useful. Uh, how do I start?

Start local. Teachers or older students in your favorite subjects can be mentors. Coaches and camp counselors can be mentors. Community leaders, accomplished aunts, and that mom down the street with the insanely cool job—all of these people make great mentors. Really, any expert in a field that you love has the potential to be a role model.

Hang on, moms and aunts? Yep, we said it. **There is something special about finding a mentor who has . . . you know, actually *been* a middle school girl and can relate to the high-tops you're standing in.** A good mentor right now is someone who understands the unique challenges facing girls as they approach high school, college, and that first day on the job. There are wise words being exchanged among women these days, and there's no reason you shouldn't strive to build your own network. Female mentors are the gold standard—find one if you can.

Whomever you select as your mentor, remember that there is a difference between a mentor and, say, a private coach or tutor, in that *mentors find mentorship relationships rewarding on their own.* They remember what it was like in the early days of their careers and are usually delighted to welcome others to the stage. Or the field. Or the lab. You get the idea. The point is you don't have to pay a mentor; they just expect you to pay it forward someday and mentor somebody else.

Lean in, girls, one last thought: as with any big step, there are important safeguards to follow. Remember to run potential mentors by the trusted adults in your life and make sure they meet each other. While gaining a mentor in middle school might be one of the most important events in your life, big middle school events usually require a parental permission slip, and this is no exception. Get everybody on board and signed off. Then you can move forward.

We know, this all sounds really grown up.

It sounds like something you shouldn't need to think about until you move out of the house and get a job. Or at least until you can drive yourself to a job. But, girls, **mentors matter, right now.**

And unlike a driver's license, you don't need to wait until high school to get one.

In fact, finding a mentor is something that will get you a whole lot further down the road than any driver's license, because the person showing you the road, well . . . she paved it.

Original version published on Huffington Post

"You are never too young to start developing your network—to seek advice/support, to connect and engage in a mentoring relationship. It's important to start having mentors and sponsors early, especially for young women. You need people thinking about you for exciting opportunities, praising your talents, and coaching you when you struggle. We advance together—make sure you invest time to build a powerful squad."

—Cate Luzio, founder and CEO of Luminary

How to Find a Mentor

Finding someone to mentor you can sound daunting at first. But the truth is that it's totally doable and also great practice for the future. *Let's break it down:*

1. HOW TO IDENTIFY A MENTOR:

Is there a particular teacher, coach, counselor, community leader, or local speaker you admire and whose focus aligns with your interests?

Do you think that person might have the time or the interest to be a mentor? Have they mentored anyone else you know?

Do your parents or other family members know this person? Do they think this person would be a wise choice as a mentor? If they don't know each other yet, make sure they meet. It's an important step!

2. HOW TO ASK:

If you've found the right person and your household is on board, then it's time to ask if they'd be interested in mentoring you. *Here are a few options:*

In person: Keep your head up, shoulders back, smile big. Shake hands, look them in the eye, and explain why you would like their guidance. Briefly state what you hope to learn and why you admire them. Then ask politely for a bit of their time and brainpower.

By email: Adopt the same confident and friendly attitude as you type, and then follow the guidelines above. When you're done—*clear throat, this is important*—check carefully for typos.

By phone: The phone can be the trickiest of the three, but if it's the only option, then go for it. Be succinct, listen well to everything the other person is saying, and then offer to follow up the conversation with an email with more details. Summarize the call in that email and propose your next steps.

Once your new mentor has agreed to grant you some time, be sure to follow up with a heartfelt thank-you. **Your efforts to make your mentor proud begin immediately.**

3. HOW TO STAY IN TOUCH:

Fast-forward a few months or years. Maybe you've moved towns, switched schools, or headed to college. Whatever the reason, you might leave the vicinity of your mentor. You want to stay in touch! *Why?* Two reasons: (1) You will never stop learning from this wise person, and (2) mentors take pride in their protégés and will want to follow your progress. *How to do this:*

Drop a periodic email to your mentor updating them on your progress. Don't let them hear about your big milestones thirdhand.

Follow your mentor on LinkedIn or other social media outlets so you can see what they're working on and follow *their* progress. Be sure to send congratulations (or cupcakes) when warranted.

When they have a big win, *cheer like crazy.* Spreading the word is not only a nice thing to do, but it keeps you and your applause emojis fresh in their mind.

The bottom line is this: mentorship relationships, if created and cultivated properly, can repay you over and over in the future. Years from now, when you're thinking about college or looking for internships, the people who knew you when you asked your first questions and incorporated your first feedback will be in your corner. They will proudly introduce you to their classmates or colleagues. They will want to see you succeed.

And you'll know exactly how to mentor the next girl.

> "My mentor provided two things that were critical in starting my career: advice and access, and I always try my best to pay that forward as a mentor to others."

—*Kellie Gerardi, aerospace and defense professional; STEM communicator; Defense Council Member, Truman National Security Project*

"IDENTIFY PEOPLE WHO DO WHAT YOU LOVE, AND LEARN FROM THEM. MENTORS MATTER . . . AS EARLY AS MIDDLE SCHOOL."

—ÊTRE

#HowToBeAMentor

Stop laughing. Seriously, just stop it. Yes, you can absolutely be a mentor in middle school!

Think you're done now that you have an awesome mentor who is inspiring and guiding you? Oh, you are so not finished! Time to pay it forward and help someone else! *Here are a few ideas to start you off:*

- Are you amazing at languages? Offer to tutor someone a few levels behind you! Does the coach always ask you to demonstrate moves on the field? Set up a pre-practice session for newer players. Look for people who want to do what you're already great at, and offer up your time to help.

- Start a mentorship club and be a founder in your school community while you help other girls.

- If someone asks you to be their mentor and you have the skills and expertise they are seeking, say yes!

Let this be a habit that extends through your life. Paying it forward is always the right thing to do. You'll get tons of satisfaction from lifting up other girls (flip back and reread that whole Shine Theory thing in chapter 1), and your own confidence will get an added boost. We promise—this is 100 percent worth it.

> "There is no right age or shape to be a role model. Keep thinking of the impact you can have and the change you can make, and create allies to help you."
>
> —*Kristy Wallace, CEO, Ellevate Network*

Mini-Mentorships: How to Schedule Your Own Lunch & Learn

About a year after Être was formed, one of the board members came up with a terrific idea. "We interview lots of amazing women by email," she said, "but it would be so cool if we could meet them." We agreed but pointed out that Être was only twelve months old and still completely under the radar. *We're too small for them to come to us,* we thought, *but maybe we can go to them.*

This one conversation started **Être's Lunch & Learns:** a series of in-person mentorship events where we take small groups of girls— ten at a time—to meet female leaders at seriously cool companies. Think Spotify, Google, NYSE, and more. We stay one hour, see their workplace, and, over a short lunch, ask all the questions we can think of.

Seriously. All. The. Questions.

You can see more about our trips and how to join the fun on our website. And **even if you don't have a Club Être chapter at your school, you could still create your own version of this!**

Having a succinct conversation with someone about what they do is like a mini-mentorship. In this scenario, just like with Être's Lunch & Learns, you're not planning an ongoing relationship; you're just learning more about where someone works and what they do. At Être, we compress our questions into an hour, trying to see and absorb as much as possible while we're on-site. The same would go for an informal convo with a role model you meet. You'll be amazed what you can learn from a few moments of focused inquiry with a fascinating subject.

And asking for ten minutes of their time just might work. Whether you ask in person, over email, or by phone, here's a simple script you can follow:

> Hi [unbelievably cool person],
>   I'm a student at [your school] in the [your grade] and I would like to learn more about [ridiculously fascinating job they have]. Would you be willing to speak with me, either in person or by phone, for ten minutes? My [parent] can accompany me if in person, and I will not stay longer than ten minutes.
>   Very sincerely,
>   [You, amazing girl]

You might get a yes. It might be scheduled very far in advance if they are busy, or they might ask for your questions by email instead, but don't worry. Either way, you'll likely get a response and maybe even some valuable answers to your questions.

OK, let's say I get the guts up to actually approach someone with a crazy cool job and they say yes . . . what are some good kinds of questions?

Glad you asked.

Here are twenty sample questions our girls have asked at various Être Lunch & Learns. Feel free to tailor or edit these to the things YOU want to know from the mentors YOU are visiting:

1. What's the best part about working at _____?

2. What makes _____ a good place or industry for women to work?

3. Does it feel weird if you are the only woman in a meeting?

4. What's something that most people don't know about _____?

5. How long have you worked at _____ and what was your path before that?

6. What classes were most important for you in school? Did you know that then?

7. What was your favorite subject in school when you were my age?

8. When you started your job here, how did you know you'd be good at it?

9. What are the skills you need most to be good at your job?

10. Who was your most important role model when you were my age?

11. Who is your most significant role model as an adult? Is it someone where you work?

12. How important is diversity (whether race, gender, nationality . . .) at _____?

13. What's the best piece of work advice you've ever received?

14. If you could go back and tell your middle school self one thing, what would it be?

15. What is a typical day like for you?

16. What motivates you more: competition *at* work or passion *about* work?

17. Was there a mistake you made at work that actually turned into an opportunity?

18. What do you think your company or industry will look like in five years? Ten years?

19. What's a work goal you haven't achieved yet?

20. What's one thing you want girls everywhere to remember?

"As I've grown up, I've begun to realize how lucky I am to have the outlook on life that I do. My mother has always taught me to embrace my mind and what I can do with it, and her words of encouragement have pushed me to be at the top of my class all throughout high school. When I look at her, I see the successful woman I one day hope to be and hope to inspire other girls to be."

—*Skylar L., Être Board member, age seventeen*

"WHILE ENGAGING WITH OTHERS IN ORDER TO LEARN AND FIND TRUTH IS IMPORTANT, THE BEST ADVICE YOU WILL EVER RECEIVE IS YOUR OWN. MENTORS CAN BEST SERVE THEIR MENTEES BY HOLDING A MIRROR UP AND LISTENING."

—*Susan Rocco, founder and host of Women to Watch Media*

"I love being granted opportunities to work with other girls who want to make a difference in the world and being inspired by women in the workplace who inspire young girls to achieve their goals."

—*Sarah G., Être Board member, age eighteen*

"Nell Merlino inspired me from the first time I met her. I remember her telling us to stop and look at ourselves in the mirror for a couple moments a day. This truly opened my eyes into realizing that I had a beautiful soul and to be comfortable with loving myself. She empowers me to be confident."

—*Michelle C., Être Board member, age seventeen*

Heard on the Bus

On the bus ride home after every Être Lunch & Learn, we hear snippets of conversations that make us smile. Actually, they make us beam because we get to hear what most impacted girls like you about a certain workplace, panel, or speaker. Whether we're on stage at **Spotify** (our very first Lunch & Learn), touring **YouTube**, learning about global finance and our place in it from leaders at **Morgan Stanley** and **Goldman Sachs**, chatting with **Google** engineers in the coolest cafeteria we have ever seen, walking onto the *TRL* set at **Viacom**, holding the gavel on the floor of the **New York Stock Exchange**, meeting Wall Street's *Fearless Girl*, or watching *Geena Davis* stand with **Marvel**, **Nat Geo**, and **Sesame Workshop** executives and speak to a packed room about gender in media, it's the words shared directly by mentors with girls that steal the show every time.

We usually include a few of these overheard quotes in our thank-you notes; here are some of the most memorable:

"She totally answered my question and another one I was going to ask, but didn't."

"I didn't know lawyers could work in places so cool."

"I'm glad we went to the stock exchange after they got a woman president!"

"I think I have the Fearless Girl*'s skirt."*

"That whole panel was women and they're all managing directors. That's boss level."

"That last speaker's entire job is to convince other women to work there. That's awesome."

"That place was so cool I'd work there for free."
   "Um, hello, whole big talk about equal pay?! No one's working for free . . . we're getting paid." (Round of high fives.)

"I have so much energy every time I get back on this bus."

"She was a badass. Can I say badass? Sorry, there's no other word for her."

"We ate lunch with four freaking Googlers."

"I would have new ideas every ten minutes if I worked in a place like that."

"There were a ton of women there. I counted."
    "Was her assistant a guy? He was, right?"

"Rocks that she walked up to someone she didn't even know in the lobby to get her job. I think I would do that."

"She said she hated raising her hand too. But she got over it at exactly my age."

Whispered to three girls crammed in the same seat— "We're going to be the people answering the questions someday."

"The Lunch & Learn trips are a way to get a head start on finding out what the world outside is really like and how you wanna shape and change it. My favorite has to be the Viacom trip because it made me realize all the incredible things there are to do in the entertainment industry and that it's something I might want to do in the near future."

—*Keren F., Être Board member, age seventeen*

"Meeting female mentors young is so important because it opens your eyes to a world that isn't always represented. From when we're little girls, we see and learn from a society that doesn't show girls being whatever they want to be or shooting for the stars. When I went to the Geena Davis conference at Google, I got to hear and meet such incredible leading women, and it made me realize there really is no limit to what us women can do. Whether it's writing a children's book or collecting wildlife data, if you can see another empowered woman do it, you know you can do it too."

—*Kayla S., Être Board member, age seventeen*

"#BeConnected—dream larger than life. Shake the hand of every person you meet. When they talk, look directly into their eyes and smile as radiantly as you can."

—*Storm G., Être Board member, age sixteen*

#BeConnected
IN TEN WORDS OR LESS:

CONNECT.
ASK QUESTIONS.
ABSORB.
MENTORS
MATTER—IN
A BIG WAY.

CHAPTER FIVE

#BeStrong

#BeStrong can mean a lot of things: sheer physical strength, sticking to your convictions, endurance, speaking up, you name it. In this chapter we focus on athleticism and competitive spirit on and off the field, as well as having the strength *not to quit* your sport! More girls than you realize leave the game between grade school and high school (you'll read about that later in the chapter), so right out of the gate, we're urging you to stay.

Stay on the field. Stay in your cleats.

Staying builds grit. Guts. A taste for greatness and a tolerance for goals missed. Characters are forged, leadership traits are honed, and teammates are elevated above individuals. CEOs looking backward would say these are skills worth staying for.

In this chapter you'll hear from some inspiring athletes facing challenges head-on, and learn about others who became change-makers after they were record-breakers. The one thing all of these athletes have in common is—you got it—they didn't quit. So keep reading. Keep playing. We'll be right here cheering.

> **"I play sports because it gives me confidence and makes me feel strong. #BeStrong."**
>
> —*Celia B., Être Board member, age fourteen*

"EXERCISE YOUR BODY AS VIGOROUSLY AS YOU EXERCISE YOUR MIND. STRETCH YOUR LIMITS. RELISH YOUR POWER. SHOW UP STRONG."

—ÊTRE

Girls, Don't Quit—Stay in Your Cleats

You love your sport.
You love your team, your captains, and your coach.
You love the win and, even more, that breathless moment before the win.
So why are you quitting?

It is a question that parents and coaches everywhere are scratching their heads about. You—our sunny, scrappy middle school athlete—seem happiest on the field. On a court. On a team. Your smile, glinting with braces, is a mile wide and your clenched fists and uplifted chin are a vision to behold. **You are strength, loyalty, and leadership rolled into one magnificent package, and you don't need cheering sidelines to know you belong out there.** So when you tell us, eyes downcast, that you are quitting . . . we are desperate to know why.

Help us understand why you are leaving something you love.

Explain why you would cut yourself from a roster you were so proud to make.

Why would a girl who never gives up on the court . . . quit?

We know you're not alone. According to the Women's Sports Foundation, by age fourteen, girls are dropping out of sports at twice the rate of boys.

Twice the rate. Of boys.

Reasons speculated include gender stereotypes, girls feeling self-conscious about their bodies, a fear of being judged, and not feeling empowered. *This is where we want to sweep everything off the kitchen table and stand on it.* But, because we want to model constructive behavior and, frankly, because standing on furniture should be reserved for more celebratory moments, we'll pull up a chair and try to explain a few things.

Namely, why you should be the exception to that statistic.

Let's start with **gender stereotypes.**

Boys are faster than girls.

Nobody wants to date the sporty girl.

OMG, gross, she's like *always* in cleats.

OK, no. Just . . . no. We don't need to tell you that boys are not always faster than girls (just ask retired soccer player Mia Hamm, who famously said, "My coach said I ran like a girl, and I said if he ran a little faster he could too"). And if the "sporty girl" is the one surrounded by her teammates, laughing and radiating joy, then trust us: everyone wants to date her. And we would rather be the strong girl in cleats than the insecure girl in wobbly heels any day of the week. *Any* day.

Now, we hear you on **the body thing.** It's a tough one. Women everywhere feel self-conscious about their bodies at one point or another, so you're definitely not alone. And middle school can be an extra tricky time. But try to look beyond the unrealistic beauty

BE THE GIRL WHO STAYS IN HER CLEATS

standards flooding your Insta feed. Instead, turn to real-life role models, like Nepal's Gaurika Singh, who, as the youngest competitor in the Rio 2016 Olympics, hopped into the pool in front of thousands of cameras at age thirteen. Or tennis player Serena Williams, who won the US Open playing while she was pregnant. Every woman has moments of insecurity, but the trick is to keep your #headinthegame. It's so worth it.

Fear of being judged. Oh, girls, if this is going to knock you off your game *now*, how will you handle raising your hand in a high school class? Sending in college applications? Nailing that first job interview?

This is a fear best overcome early, and being surrounded by a supportive team is just the place to start. Yes, your coach may scream directions from the bench in a less than helpful manner. And yes, some bleacher parents may display a startling *lack* of manners. **But showing up with a strong backbone and a**

thick skin is as important as remembering your shin guards. Bring your game, your equipment, and a firm resolve to play your best no matter what the sidelines say. Suiting up like this will serve you well in any locker room, classroom, or boardroom.

And now, the most important part—feeling empowered. Stop for a minute and think about how you feel when you are standing in that goal. Poised under the basket. Reaching high to serve. Stretching toward the finish line. In that suspended moment before the game-winning, clock-stopping, net-skimming play, *how do you feel?*

Yep, that's empowerment.

That's playing your position and owning the moment. If you need proof, watch the riveting #WhenIPlay video from our heroes at espnW and let the words hang in the air: *"When I play, I know who I am."*

You know who you are, because you know what you can do. Regardless of how you felt at the first tryout or grueling practice, in that moment when you are *truly* in the game, you know you can do anything. And the more you play, the more you will feel that. The more you grow, train, and align yourself with your team and the rhythm of the game, the more you'll understand how powerful you can be.

And you need to stick with it.

It's not just that regular exercise is good for you (although a recent report noted that fewer than one-third of kids today are "active to a healthy level"). And it's not only because girls with good sportsmanship are more likely to be valued team members in the workplace (although an EY/espnW global study of female executives showed sports to be a clear indicator of leadership and career achievement).

It's that you should always stay true to the things you love. Developing an authentic sense of yourself means recognizing the things that bring you joy and finding ways to keep them in your life. Yes, it takes balance. Yes, it takes confidence. No question, it requires prioritizing. But *you know what you love . . .* and it's up to you to keep it up.

Girls, don't quit.

Stay in your cleats.

So much more than the score depends on it.

Original version published on Huffington Post

"I think it's important for girls not to quit their sports, because constantly getting after your goals and finally achieving them is such a wonderful feeling. When I joined the wrestling team, I made it my goal to show the boys and my coaches that I *do* belong and I *can* do everything, if not better than the rest of them. With hard work and determination, it motivated me, and toward the end of the season, I know for a fact that I proved it to them."

—Anna S., Être Board member, age seventeen

Sports Stats:

Here are some super valuable sports stats you need to know, straight out of the EY/espnW *Where Will You Find Your Next Leader?* report:

Ninety-four percent of women in the C-suite played sports.

FIFTY-TWO PERCENT OF C-SUITE WOMEN PLAYED SPORTS AT THE UNIVERSITY LEVEL, COMPARED TO 39 PERCENT OF WOMEN AT OTHER MANAGEMENT LEVELS.

Seventy-seven percent of C-suite women think women who played sports make good employees.

So. Many. Numbers. And, um, what's a C-suite? C-suite generally refers to the top jobs at organizations; jobs that start with chief (chief executive officer or CEO, chief financial officer or CFO).

Wait, so that report says women at the top think sports helped them get there? **Yes.**

Wow. Exactly.

Ê-Interview with NASCAR racer (and STEM advocate) Julia Landauer

Stop everything. Have you met Être role model *NASCAR* driver **Julia Landauer**? Since making history as the first and youngest female champion in the Skip Barber Race Series at age fourteen (*let that sink in . . . we'll be right here),* Julia has amassed dozens of wins in tons of different racing series! But here's the coolest part . . . while collecting all these NASCAR wins, Julia is also using her racing platform to encourage #girlsinSTEM! Read Être's interview with Julia below, follow her on social everywhere @julialandauer, and get as fired up as we are!

Ê: *After winning a NASCAR Track Championship in 2015, being the highest finishing female in the K&N series history, and being the only female member of the NASCAR Next class of 2016–2017, do you still get nervous before big races like these? Does being a woman make you more or less nervous . . . or does it not make any difference at all?*

JL: I always get nervous before races! If I don't feel nervous, that means I'm not mentally in the right space. Everyone invests so much time and effort and energy into racing, and I approach each race with the sole purpose of winning. It's very nerve-racking in the best way. I don't think being a woman makes a difference in nerve levels. **I think most great athletes feel some kind of nerves before competition.**

Ê: *You were really close to our age when you became the first (and youngest) female champion in the Skip Barber Race Series at age fourteen—what would you tell girls today who are fascinated by racing but, because of our age, don't get a chance to learn about it? How can girls get more exposure to racing or start competing at a young age?*

JL: I think the key to getting involved in anything is to do your homework about it: research it, read magazines, read online articles, there are books on racing, et cetera. The thing that sets racing apart from a lot of other sports is the high cost to compete, but there are groups that give scholarships and grants

to girls in sports and girls in motorsports. I also think it's important to reach out to the people/adults around you for help. If your parents aren't the right people, then maybe teachers or counselors or aunts/uncles, people who can help with all of the logistics and planning. Never be afraid to ask for help!

Ê: *You also graduated from Stanford, where you studied science and tech, and we heard you have a huge interest in STEM. How does STEM intersect with racing, and what advice do you have for motivated girls who love STEM subjects but don't always have access to the right resources? Do you have any favorite STEM challenges that would be appropriate for girls our age?*

JL: Racing is a technology-centric sport, we're literally maneuvering machines to make them go as fast as possible. There's a lot of physics, chemistry, engineering, and mechanics that go into building a race car, setting it up properly, and driving it. As drivers we have to give feedback for what we want changed on the car, and the crew chief / lead engineer has to translate that into technical changes the mechanics have to make. It's really cool!

As for getting involved, I'd recommend doing research on what programs your school may have for STEM fields, what camps you could attend, what camps have scholarships (e.g., Girls Who Code), and look into tech kits that you can find in stores. If your school doesn't have a club in place for the type of STEM subjects you want to work on, suggest they start one! It's important to take initiative and create something where you think there might be a void.

"Don't focus on the tough days or the losses. Stay out there, whatever you are doing. After all, everything heals better in fresh air, and the next day is always around the corner. #BeStrong."

—*Kenzie P., Être Board member, age seventeen*

"GIRLS, FOLLOW YOUR HEART, SHOOT FOR THE STARS AND THE GOAL."

—Sophie M., Être Board
Member, age twelve

Record-Breakers and Changemakers

Being strong on the middle school field can generate lifelong strength in other areas of your life. Right now it might seem like next week's scrimmage or—*fingers crossed*—the championship season is as far into the future as you can see. But the teamwork and leadership skills you are gaining are character traits that will take you far and help you have an impact bigger than you can imagine.

In fact, successful athletes are some of the most impactful activists out there. Meet a few of these barrier-breaking

champions who are proudly using their strength and voice to further important causes. **Because**—*cue national anthem music*—**platforms aren't just for receiving medals, girls. They're for standing on to create lasting change.**

We like examples.

OK, the next time you feel cornered by a gym-locker bully or cyber-crushed on social, remember that three-time Olympic gold medalist **Gabby Douglas** was openly bullied online during the Rio 2016 Olympic Games. Haters mocked her hair, facial expressions, and hand gestures to such an extent that she left social media altogether until after she won the gold. *At which point*, she vaulted back hard (sorry), teaming up with Intel, Vox, Recode, and Lady Gaga's Born This Way Foundation to become the first Change Ambassador for their #HackHarassment project.

Want another? Listen to **Abby Wambach** when she speaks about breaking through limits and fighting for comprehensive equal pay. *Wait, two-time Olympic gold medalist, FIFA*

World Cup champion, and all-time highest goal scorer for male and female soccer players globally Abby Wambach? Yup. Based on her graduation speech at Barnard College in 2018 that went completely viral, Abby's platform Wolfpack is now encouraging women and girls everywhere to ditch old rules and change the game.

Other female athletes are changing the game just by opening new doors. *Think* Rubab Raza, who, at age thirteen, became the first Pakistani female Olympic swimmer in 2004 (50-meter freestyle) and Lubna Al-Omair, who became the first female fencer to represent Saudi Arabia at the Olympics in 2016 (individual foil)—both big firsts! And tennis legend Billie Jean King, winner of thirty-nine Grand Slam singles, doubles, and mixed doubles titles, including—*you're not even ready*—a record twenty Wimbledon titles, founded the Women's Sports Foundation in 1974 to ensure *all* girls open doors and access to sports. In each of these cases, **athletes used their spotlight in sports to further a larger cause.** We'll play on that team all day long.

"Female athletes have an ability to assess risk and be perhaps a little bit more bold than a lot of other women. Don't hide that. That is going to be very useful."

—Claire Shipman, *bestselling coauthor of* The Confidence Code for Girls

The New and Inclusive Friday Night Lights

Being strong takes on a whole new meaning for differently abled athletes. We are huge fans of multisport events like the **Paralympics** and the **Special Olympics**, as well as single-sport organizations like **The Sparkle Effect**. Meet **Sarah Cronk, founder of The Sparkle Effect**, who launched this inclusive cheer program when she was a *sophomore in high school. Wait, you'll go hoarse with the cheering.*

Ê: *How old were you when you started The Sparkle Effect, and how did it come to be?*

SC: In 2008, **when I was fifteen**, I helped to create the nation's first school-based cheer team designed to bring together students with and without disabilities, the Pleasant Valley High School Spartan Sparkles. My initial interest in inclusion stemmed from my relationship with my brother, who has a developmental disability. After creating the Spartan Sparkles, I realized that students nationwide could start their own inclusive cheer and dance teams, which is why I created The Sparkle Effect in 2009. Since then, **over ten thousand students** have directly participated on two hundred teams in thirty-one states.

Ê: *Why do you think your mission of total inclusivity resonates with a sport like cheerleading, which can sometimes be thought of as overly exclusive?*

SC: I have loved turning the cheerleader stereotype on its head through The Sparkle Effect. Cheerleading, at its core, is about school spirit. It's about rooting for each other, even when the chips are down. **It's about rallying our communities around a common cause. To me, there's nothing more inclusive than that.** Cheerleading as an activity is also incredibly adaptive—it can be modified to suit any skill level. The public nature of cheerleading also has allowed us to put a bright spotlight on inclusion—to show audiences nationwide what individuals with disabilities can do and the many ways in which we're more alike than different.

Ê: *How did you know that a sports program started by a high school student (totally youth-driven and youth-led) would turn into a national program with over two hundred teams? What was the "ah-ha" moment, when you knew it could grow and be scaled like that?*

SC: I can't say that I ever did know! I've been at this for ten years now, and I still pinch myself every day. The first time the Sparkles team at my high school took the field, I knew we were on to something special. The impact the team was making on our community indicated to me that the idea was worth sharing. But I was definitely figuring things out as I went along. My initial goal was to create one hundred teams, and in our first year we only generated two. I went through many years of trying and failing, and pivoting and trying again. **All I really knew was that I couldn't give up.**

Ê: *Did the success of your team change any other sports at your school? Have you* heard of other sports picking up on your *inclusivity mission to make similar changes at other schools?*

SC: Yes! When I was in high school, it was a real struggle for my brother to be accepted into any school activities. There was even an issue about him joining the school choir, even though he has perfect pitch. It's important to keep in mind most authority figures in American high schools grew up in an era when people with disabilities were completely segregated from the rest of the population. Seeing the Sparkles on game night was **the first time most folks in our school and community had seen social inclusion in action**. Once both students and adults saw how simple and easy inclusion is, everything at our school started to transform. **Now, students with disabilities are welcome everywhere— in choir, theater, sports, you name it.** The transformation has become [so] ingrained that most people in the community genuinely can't imagine it being any other way.

Ê: *Besides the very real and intensive "Friday night lights" cheer experience, what else do Sparkle Effect team members gain in terms of mentorship, leadership, and empowerment opportunities?*

SC: We've always said that **"when everyone cheers, everyone wins,"** because we believe that everyone involved in a Sparkle Effect team benefits from the experience. Students with disabilities report improved confidence and social skills. Students without disabilities describe the experience of being on a Sparkle Effect team as life changing, and report that their involvement has given them a sense of purpose. Parents say that their involvement has helped them feel less marginalized. They find gratification in being able to attend events where their children are participating and in seeing their children form genuine friendships with their peers, sometimes for the first time. And through the years, we see **entire communities** more readily embrace inclusion as a way of being.

> ## "I started martial arts at the age of ten, so I can definitely say – stay with what you love. Don't be influenced by outside noise . . . it's most important to be happy with who you are."
>
> *—Michelle Waterson, MMA fighter with UFC*

"I have found my deepest morality and greatest achievements through sports. The playing field was my first teacher of determination, tenacity, and resilience. The wins and losses were my second teachers of grace. When faced with adversity now, I think back to the days I trained harder than anyone else, and that's what helps me get back up again and again."

—MARYSOL CASTRO, FIRST FEMALE PUBLIC ADDRESS (PA) ANNOUNCER FOR THE NEW YORK METS AND FIRST LATINA PA ANNOUNCER IN MAJOR LEAGUE BASEBALL

Ê-Interview with Dr. Jen Welter— First Female NFL Coach

Making Friday night lights shine even brighter, meet **Dr. Jen Welter**! The first female NFL coach *and* the first female running back, Coach Jen is a two-time gold medalist *(with a PhD in psych)* who wanted to see more girls on the field. Girls like YOU. Read how she founded **Grrridiron Girls** and what she wants you to know about #kickingglass.

Ê: *Lots of girls know that you were the first female NFL coach (Arizona Cardinals—so*

cool), but not everyone knows that you were also the first female to play running back *in men's pro football (even cooler!). What was that like and why was it such an important glass ceiling to break?*

JW: Football has often been referred to as the final frontier for women in sports, so for me, I believed if we could change football, we could change the world. What better place to show that women could literally tackle anything, in football and in life, right? I didn't have a grand plan of playing men's football or coaching in the NFL—those were things that had not happened, so I didn't even dream it was possible. Actually, when I made my first football team, I just made a promise to myself that I would step up to whatever challenge the game put in my way. I had no idea how big those challenges would be! But I just kept following the game with that mentality. Each "kick glass" moment was especially important because it gave permission to girls to dream bigger than I ever did.

Playing with the guys was amazing. We all became better versions of ourselves through that and became really tight in a situation that everyone assumed would fail. They looked out for me on the field, and I looked out for them off the field. We became so close that it actually caught the attention of the new head coach the following season, and he offered me a coaching position.

Ê: *We love that you play and coach, but what we also really love are your flag football camps for girls! How did these get started, and what's your ultimate goal?*

JW: When I made it to the NFL, there were girls (just like you) who reached out to me from all over the world and sent pictures with footballs and letters thanking me for giving them permission to be different. Obviously, being the first, I knew how it felt to be different, and I actually realized what makes me different makes me special. I wanted all those girls to know that they were special too. I tried to post and share their stories as much as possible, but I knew I wanted to do more.

When I finished in the NFL, I was coaching camps all over the country, and I realized none of them were for girls! So I decided I wanted to do them. I thought everyone would see what I saw, but they didn't! Believe it or not, everyone told me it wouldn't work. Well, thankfully, I am used to proving people wrong, so with just a few people who believed in me and no sponsors, I announced a national tour. In our first year, we did nineteen camps in fifteen cities.

Our philosophy of Grrridiron Girls is "showing girls there is no game you cannot play, and no field you do not belong in or on." Teaching confidence through football. I want girls to know everything is possible, they can do everything the boys can when the opportunities are open and the coaching is provided. I want Grrridiron Girls to represent every girl who tackles her dreams, and that we have leagues and games domestically and internationally.

Ê: *So many girls quit their sports in middle school, and we're always urging girls to "stay in their cleats." What would you say to girls our age to convince them to stay on the field and in their sport?*

JW: We love you. We see you. We want you. You belong. And . . . the future is bright for girls in sports. There are doors opening every day because there are women kicking glass for you. I was working on the "keep playing like a girl" campaign, and I heard three stats:

7 out of 10 girls feel like they don't belong in sports;

7 out of 10 girls feel like society doesn't support them in sports; and

5 out of 10 girls will opt out of sports by the time they finish puberty.

To me, that was a call to action; I knew if I was not that woman, that visible female role model who was hands on with you and working to give you better, then the wrong woman was the first female coach in the NFL . . . girls, everything that made me wrong by certain standards and outdated thinking is what actually made me right. Get out there and go after what you want. Have fun.

#BeStrong
IN TEN WORDS OR LESS:

GIRLS, STAY
IN YOUR
CLEATS.
YOU BELONG
ON THE FIELD.

CHAPTER SIX

#BeInformed

Be the girl who knows what's going on. Be the girl who gets her news from multiple platforms (we're talking email, social, podcasts, papers, *and* TV) and from a deep bench of sources. You can't really call yourself informed if you're listening to only one channel or reading one site. Seriously, that just makes you a fan.

And you're so much more than that. You're the girl who digs for facts. Who seeks out statistics to back up the sound bites. You want your news to have verified status.

This chapter is all about finding reliable news sources and discovering ways to broaden your view. Because when you're informed, you can become a better leader. Think you can't learn about politics because you're too young to vote? Think again. There are lots of female-driven political orgs on both sides of the aisle that offer resources specifically geared to girls your age. Want to know more about climate change, immigration, and other top issues of the day? Want to learn about women in politics and the path to get there? Yeah, you do. Be the girl in the know. Start here.

"Be the girl who votes her future."

—Être

Watch the News . . . but Know Your Own Mind

There's. Just. So. Much. News.
Why is it always "breaking"?
Why is everyone yelling?
Why should I even listen?

Oh, middle school girls—we know. Parents tell you to be informed, and then we sit you in front of split screens of interrupting adults. Teachers urge you to follow current events, and your newsfeed overflows with outrage. Substance gets overtaken by snark, and headlines become hashtags before you can even read the original article.

You want to be the girl who knows what's going on.

BE THE GIRL *with* HER OWN VIEWS

But it's hard to do when the information flow is never-ending and polarizing to the point of that *the-dinner-table-will-actually-freaking-explode-if-anyone-brings-up-the-news* feeling.

So you stay quiet, avoiding words like *investigation, gun control, peace talks,* and *climate change.* You scroll past the all-caps tirades, resting instead on safer posts about #NationalTacoDay. We know. We love tacos a ridiculous amount.

But we also know that you care about the world around you.

And other people know it too. Research from Common Sense Media tells us that following the news is important to today's kids. We see you catching glimpses of the updates that crawl across the bottom of the TV screen and stream down your social feeds. *That's all kinds of good.* It means the wheels in that bright head of yours are turning. It means curiosity is flickering. Ideas are forming.

Here's what we want you to remember:

The world is big.

And the well of information you draw from should be big too.

When you watch the news, try to watch a *variety of news sources*, not just the channel your family watches.

When you research world events for homework, branch out and *read across a multitude of platforms*, not just the media found in your classroom.

When you listen to experts, listen to *as many different voices as possible*, not just those held captive in the bubble of your Twitter feed.

Because here's the inside scoop: **your parents' views on an issue might not necessarily be your views.** This goes for your teachers, coaches, and club leaders. Even a mentor, your favorite one, might have an opinion that doesn't exactly match up with yours.

Girls, that's OK.

Diversity of thought is *good.*

Varied perspectives are *important.*

Being well informed today means seeing the big picture, seeking out reliable facts, and listening to smart people. Like, *lots* of them. You don't have to agree with a view to learn from it, and having a deep bench of opposing ideas can actually help clarify your own beliefs.

The point is to focus on the issues and **decide what resonates with you.** Gaining independence at this age isn't only about chores and privileges. It's about developing your own thoughts and cultivating your own core beliefs.

This is all part of growing up.

And you are coming of age in a critical time.

Important decisions are being made around the world that will matter to you for a very long time. Think education, health care, the environment, and basic human rights. Luckily, there are plenty of resources to keep you and your friends squarely in the loop. In the know. In a position to argue for fairness and fight for justice when you are ready.

Listen to it all, girls.

Resist the urge to hit mute or scroll forward. **You can't be truly informed if you listen only to stuff that sounds familiar.** Be brave enough to seek out media with a fresh outlook and people with thought-provoking views. You're smart. You're figuring out what you believe.

So be that girl.

The one who listens to everyone—but knows her own mind.

Original version published on Huffington Post

"Defending yourself before listening to others doesn't make you strong; it makes you stubborn. Listening to the other side of the story always forces you to get out of your bubble. #BeInformed."

—*Tanvi C., Être Board member, age seventeen*

Age-Appropriate Resources for Staying Informed

It's so important to keep your fingers on the pulse of what's happening in the world. Here are some of Être's favorite sites to help you do just that. Check 'em out. Note their differences. Keep an ear out for varied opinions, and then start forming your own.

YOUR BASIC GOTTA-KNOW-WHAT'S-HAPPENING NEWS:

PBS NewsHour Extra: This site spotlights valuable resources for seventh to twelfth graders. It includes student-generated news videos plus a "Student Voices" section, where you could be published!

Smithsonian TweenTribune: National news, odd news, teens in the news—anything from the general to the super obscure is featured here. *Extra credit:* The site is filtered by grade level, from middle to high school, so everyone is covered.

TIME for Kids: Highlighting top stories cut down to size and sorted by topic, this site is a good resource for a quick recap of the latest news. Check out tags like *World*, *Environment*, or *Young Game Changers* when you have to research something specific or especially newsy.

AND SOME EXTRA NEWS ON CLIMATE CHANGE, BECAUSE . . . SCIENCE:

NASA Climate Kids: A handy site featuring up-to-the-minute info on climate change developments. Don't miss their *NASA Wavelength* for a great guide to all of their earth and science resources.

Nat Geo Climate Change: This site gets right to the basics: What's *exactly* causing climate change, and what are the effects? The site has everything you need to know about the warming planet, what's at stake, and what you can do to help.

What Recent Elections Teach Middle School Girls

You hear it in the background on TV in the morning. Sound bites on your way to school about "firsts" and "waves." Someone mentioned something about the youngest woman elected to Congress in . . . ever.

Right. What does this all mean?

It means, girls, that leadership is redefining itself. It's starting earlier, growing more diverse, and—specifically—showing up female. Elections are getting a tiny bit cooler lately. And this matters for you.

It matters because not only are women running in record numbers, but they are winning and making history. (Need proof? According to Rutgers, in the 2018 midterms, 16 women ran for governor, 23 ran for Senate, and 233 ran for the House. Records, all. Oh, and 3,418 women ran for state legislatures.) **More women are being elected to the House than ever before, which means there are more decision-makers and role models who** *look like you.*

This is where being informed comes into play. Looking up to these women shows that leadership comes in all sizes, shapes, colors, and genders. It shows that leadership isn't just about catchy slogans and charisma; it's about being prepared and informed. The women running and winning today know what it takes to #BeInformed and what to do from there in order to lead.

Watch them. Learn from them. Now, let's get you ready *to be* them.

Five Quick Leadership Takeaways for Informed Girls:

1. **Leadership isn't luck.** Leadership is about preparation, hard work, and accentuating your unique skills. It isn't about flash and chance. It's about homework and effort. Leaders aren't lucky, girls . . . they're qualified and ready.

2. **Leaders are listeners.** True leaders listen actively and make sure even the quietest members around them are heard. Eye contact and empathy replace cynicism (and they're probably

not scrolling through their phones while constituents are talking). Leaders listen to learn.

3. **Leaders are helpers.** Not only do valued leaders listen, they remember what they've heard so that they know how to help. *That's* how a difference is made. Asking "What can I do?" isn't just polite—it is powerful and produces change.

4. **Leaders aren't perfect.** Nope, they're not. In fact, many impactful leaders lost their first time around. But a true leader owns their mistakes, learns valuable lessons along the way, and tries again.

5. **Leaders lead from anywhere.** What we mean here is that leadership doesn't have to exist on a large scale. You can lead from even the smallest places—the front of the morning assembly, the back of the class, the end of the bench—and you can start at any time.

Like, now. Start now.

Leaders who look a lot like you are standing up and defying expectations. They got there by working hard, listening well, and looking for ways to help. They picked issues, big and small, that needed a champion. And they just got started.

And, girls, all of them were once in middle school—just like you—eager to make a difference but uncertain how to begin. **They were leaders . . . they just didn't know it yet.**

But now you do. And you're ready. **Listen, learn, and lead.**

Original version published on Medium; republished by Ellevate

"No matter who you are, where you are, and what you want to be . . . just know you will make an impact on someone."

—*Avery E., Être Board member, age fifteen*

"FOR GIRLS WHO WANT TO RAISE AWARENESS, GIVE FACTS AND NUMBERS INSTEAD OF JUST EMOTION. THIS DOESN'T MEAN BOTTLE UP YOUR FEELINGS . . . BUT BACK THEM UP WITH FACTS."

—ADRIANNE HASLET, BOSTON MARATHON BOMBING SURVIVOR, BALLROOM DANCER, BLADE RUNNER, GLOBAL ACTIVIST FOR AMPUTEE RIGHTS

Ready to Run?

Now that you're ready to lead, check out these sites geared toward encouraging young women to run for office or volunteer with a campaign. *Looking. Directly. At. You.*

She Should Run: Focused purely on inspiring women and girls to run for political office, *She Should Run* wants girls just like you to get involved, get connected, and get ready to be on a ballot! As they say: *#YouCanBeAnything*.

Run for Something: This organization is designed to recruit and support talented progressives for roles in government. Think young, scrappy outsiders jumping in the political ring. Sound like you?

Running Start: This nonpartisan group has trained over twelve thousand young women to lead in politics! Check out their alum showcases, their Young Women to Watch Awards, and their awesome #ILookLikeAPolitician movement!

All In Together: Picture an amazing nonpartisan organization committed to finding innovative solutions to advance the progress of women's political and civic leadership in the US. Now picture great research and articles from news sources as varied as *CNN*, *Fox*, *Forbes*, and *Marie Claire*—all designed to keep you in the loop and someday on the ticket!

IGNITE: Building a pipeline of young women ready to be the next generation of political leaders, this nonpartisan and inspirational org will inspire you to action.

Girls in Politics: With nonpartisan programs like Camp Congress, Camp UN, and Camp Parliament across the US for girls ages eight to seventeen, our smart friends at #GIP know it all and will get you ready to run! Bonus: Their *Empower Your Daughter* guides and tool kits are *made* for you!

Getting Today's Girls on Tomorrow's Ballots

You've heard us say it before, girls: raise your hands *(pause—flip to chapter 1—come right back)*. Raise your hands in class, in support of what you believe, and in protest of what you disavow. But there's yet another reason for you to raise those hands: to run. For office.

You know that feeling when you solve a friend's problem? Or pitch in to help a neighbor? The glow that comes from making a difference? What if you could feel that way all the time? As part of your job?

Well, you can.

BE THE GIRL WITH DREAMS. BIG ONES.

Public service, at every level, offers the opportunity for accomplishment and actual change. And—*wait for it*—you don't need to be a grown-up to start.

Running for student council or class president can help bring fresh initiatives to your school. Listening to political speeches or debates can help you decide how you feel about current issues and get you ready to run. Volunteering puts you in the room.

Because here's the thing: you want to be the girl in the room where things are being decided.

Always.

And while women are making huge strides in political leadership, as we've already covered in this chapter, **there's still a lot of work to be done.**

Here's the bad news: Women don't make up *even close to half* of the US political process. *Not close to half.* Right now, less than 24 percent of the US Congress is female, and only three of our nine Supreme Court justices are women. *Hang on . . . it gets more depressing.* Women today make up only 29 percent of US state legislators, hold fewer than 30 percent of statewide elected executive offices, and represent merely 27 percent of the mayors in the one hundred largest US cities . . . and the numbers are even smaller for women of color.

This is why we need YOU.

And here's the good news: You have an army of supporters already at your back, from those in your own home to those in charge of the political pipelines. A research survey from She Should Run indicates that today's parents see their daughters as natural-born leaders and, despite the gender gap in politics, believe in their ability to succeed. And CEOs of today's political organizations believe in you too. Listen when Girls In Politics founder **Kimberly Mitchem-Rasmussen** reminds you that you have a voice:

> *You have a voice and it matters. You are fortunate in that technology, specifically social media, allows you the opportunity to amplify your voice and mobilize not just the girls in your community but girls around the world. Take advantage of this opportunity and speak out on the issues that you care about most. You have a voice and it matters.*

Then hear what **Lauren Leader-Chivee**, cofounder and CEO of All In Together, wants you to know:

> *The voting age may be eighteen, but that doesn't mean you need to wait until then to actively engage with politics. Whether it's attending town halls, writing letters to elected representatives, or campaigning for a local candidate, there are so many ways that girls of any age can advocate for the issues they care about. Research shows that women are less likely than men to participate in political advocacy. Girls—we need your voices and your passion to help change that!*

We need you.
We need you to raise your hand and raise your voice.

Because sooner than you realize, you'll be the girl in the voting booth, and then maybe, *just maybe*, the woman on the ballot.

Original version published on Huffington Post

> "Calibrate to your own strengths. Lean in to what feels natural to you. Engage your vision of leadership . . . not what you think 'leaders' look like."
>
> —*Neha Gandhi, Editor in Chief and COO at Girlboss*

"Be unapologetically yourself."

—Franki G., Être Board Member, age fifteen

Checklist for Running a Strong Student Council Campaign:

Maaaaaybe your first elected office isn't so far away! Seriously, think about it. What about starting with your school?

First of all, no. How would I even do that?

We've got you. Think of this section as a virtual campaign manager. Let's start. The main thing is running for student council requires not just ideas about what your school needs but a clear sense of your strengths and weaknesses and a willingness to ask for help. Knowing that you are not great at spelling or can't draw a straight line, for example, means you may want to enlist helpers for posters. If giving a speech makes you think *hard pass*, keep reading. We've included a quick checklist of things to consider before you run for student office, and the kind of awesome team you'll want to pull around you. And just think, when you ultimately run for higher office (*see what we did there*), maybe you'll put one or two of these

teammates on your staff. You never know.

1. **Do you have the time to run?** Think schoolwork, sports, guitar lessons, and your dog-walking job. Can you meet all of your other obligations and still take this on? If not, what can be moved around? Give this some thought and discuss it with your parents. *Ê-NOTE:* Do not bail on the dog.

2. **Do you meet the school requirements to run?** Are your grades in line, do you have too many late passes (we're not judging), can you meet the deadlines by which forms must be submitted? Make sure you satisfy all school rules for the position you want before proceeding.

3. **Do you have a platform?** Assuming you check off the first two items, think about why you want to run. What do you want to

change? What issues are top of mind for your grade, and how will you address them? Make a list and see what sparks your interest and if you can identify real ways to make changes during the school year. This will become the distinguishing platform of your campaign.

4. **Do you have to give a speech, and are you cool with that?** Some people are effortless public speakers—they stride to the stage, grab the mic, and just start talking. If this is you, awesome. *Skip to 5*. If you're more the type to *vomit in her locker* at the thought of a speech, though, you're in good company. Lots of people don't enjoy this part, but here's another occasion where asking for help pays off. Find a teacher you trust and get some coaching. Watch kids giving TED-Ed talks on YouTube and observe how they pace themselves. A little practice and a lot of courage will help you conquer your fear of public speaking, a clear win for the rest of your (political) life . . . and your locker.

5. **Let's talk art and slogans.** Have artistic friends or clever writers who can pitch in? Now's the time to call them. You need a catchy slogan that blows people's minds without breaking school rules. Then, poster the place. See if you are allowed to engage with classmates over social media. If yes, create a campaign hashtag. Keep it clean, inject some wit, and always tie it back to your campaign issues.

6. **Wait, what issues?** *We just talked about this!* The *issues* are the real reason you are running in this thing. Pick issues that mean something to you and that affect your school community. It's easy, sometimes, to pick global issues that sound familiar and important. But remember, you are running for school office, so the solutions you are proposing need to be school-centered. Save your soaring rhetoric and global peace plan for when you run for mayor. Or Congress. We'll be ready to help. With way more than posters.

"If you love what you're doing, stick with it and work hard. Keep your drive . . . and beat the boys while you're at it!"

—*Anjali Forber-Pratt, PhD, Paralympic medalist and Assistant Professor, Vanderbilt*

#BEINFORMED
IN TEN WORDS OR LESS:

BE THE GIRL IN THE KNOW.

READ. REFLECT. RUN.

CHAPTER SEVEN

#BeCharitable

Here is what this chapter is *not* going to do. It's not going to tell you that you have to spearhead a charity drive that makes zillions of dollars in order to have any kind of impact. It's not going to tell you that bake sales solve everything. (Cupcakes help, though. Not gonna lie.)

You—the empathetic and globally aware girl—already know the importance of giving back. What you want now is a map of how to get there. So, what this chapter *will* do is suggest a bunch of causes that might resonate with you and then guide you step by step toward getting involved. Without needing a car or a checkbook, and armed only with your smarts and a giant heart, you will discover actionable ways to #BeCharitable in middle school. This chapter will also spotlight helpful charity finders (so you can search for organizations by topic in your area), cool new giving apps, and short exercises to help clarify your plan of action.

It's time to give, girls. Give time and skill. Give with your friends. Give with everything you've got.

> "Be the girl who opens her heart, exceeds her goals, rallies her friends, and makes an impact."
>
> —*Être*

Be the Girl Who Inspires Giving

Not the one who only posts about the charities her favorite celebs are promoting.

Not the one who Insta-likes every nonprofit but actually learns about none of them.

Nope. Be the girl who dives deeply into a cause she cares about and discovers the kind of difference she can truly make.

The world needs that girl right now.

Here's the thing: A lot of kids get volunteering wrong. They wake up one day, realize they need community service credits for school, and reach for the closest cause. It's usually a nonprofit supported by their parents, or the top trending charity on Twitter. What it's usually not is a reflection of their core interests.

That doesn't make it a bad choice, necessarily—just a less personal one. And giving usually works best when the cause moves you.

So, what do you love? What incites your fervor? Hunger relief? Environmental protection? Animal rescue? There is no right answer, and there are seriously millions of organizations from which to choose. If you're overwhelmed, websites like Charity Navigator or VolunteerMatch are great places to start. This is worth thinking about carefully because once you begin, you'll spend valuable hours and precious energy working for the cause you pick.

Make sure you select something close to your heart.

Once you've picked a cause to champion, it's time to inspire others to join you. And, girls, this is where you will shine. Admit it, you already play at the varsity level when it comes to rallying your friends. Shift your social media prowess into high gear here and #spreadtheword. Let your followers know that there is a problem you think needs solving. Draw attention to organizations working on the issues that speak to you. Remember, you don't have to be the girl that donates all the funds (we promise the adults can handle that part). *Right now, you can be the girl who highlights the need and moves others to action.*

Because being philanthropic is important. And as you head into high school and college, it's only going to get more important. A few years ago, Harvard University published a report urging students to "engage in forms of service that are authentically chosen." Dozens of other colleges agreed. This doesn't mean open your calendars and your hearts because Harvard said so.

But **Harvard has a point—charitable efforts should start young, last long, and stay true to what you love.** In fact, Harvard updated this report in light of recent college admissions scandals and came to *the same conclusion again*, emphasizing that "What makes service meaningful and what matters to the deans is whether service is chosen based on authentic interest, and is immersive, meaningful and sustained." *Cue campus cheer.*

So be the girl who inspires authentic giving. And start now.

For the sake of . . . everything, be that girl.

Original version published on Thrive Global

"Mahatma Gandhi once said: 'The best way to find yourself is to lose yourself in the service of others.' I have been doing community service and helping younger kids in and outside of school, and it always makes me feel happy. When I'm able to help the younger kids with their homework or reading, I feel like I can do so much more than is expected of teenagers. It feels good when they look up to me too."

—*Lily O., Être Board member, age fourteen*

Helpful Charity Finders

Got it. But how do I find a cause that matters to me?

A charity finder does exactly what it sounds like: it helps you locate charities that neatly fit your age, location, and interests. Whether they're called charity finders, volunteer locators, or service coordinators, the following organizations do a terrific job matching you with ways to give. *Ê–NOTE:* Most of these require users to be thirteen or older, or to have a parent or guardian reading alongside them. So grab a household grown-up and take a spin through a few of our favorites:

Charity Navigator: Helps you make smarter choices about giving by vetting and rating each charity. They have top 10 lists (10 Charities Worth Watching), hot topics, and a blog! Check them out to give smarter.

VolunteerMatch: Brings people and causes together by matching you up with your ideal charity. You can search by topic, country, skills, and more, or just browse to see what's out there. An awesome organization with a huge impact.

TeenLife: Lists volunteer opportunities for students in grades 7 to 12; also offers lots of other valuable resources. Scroll to "Volunteer Opportunities" to see what kind of impact you can make through their community service programs.

Points of Light: Dedicated to volunteer service, this org offers detailed searching by location or issue. Head to their "Get Involved" tab to search for volunteer opportunities—you'll be amazed by what you find.

BE THE GIRL *with* FOLLOW THROUGH

Mmmmkay . . . So Now What? What Can I Actually Do?

A lot. Don't kid yourself! Philanthropy is an area where lots of people blatantly underestimate girls your age. They think it's sweet that you want to give back and they tell you so; then they glance at each other over your head and make that *isn't-she-the-most-adorable* face. You've seen it.

Ah, but **you are not adorable so much as you are powerful**. And you have the capacity to give back in a meaningful way. You feel passionately about certain causes, and you have the time and energy to spend. What you don't exactly have yet is a direction. This section is here to help.

Below is a word cloud with a sampling of worthy causes. **Circle any that interest you— or write in your own—and then answer the questions that follow.** This exercise will help you narrow your focus and start on a path that you can follow throughout middle and high school, and beyond.

Military Service Members
Mental Health
Children
International Crises
Social Justice
Refugee Aid
Clean Water
Literacy
Disaster Relief
Animal Rescue
Disability
Art
Faith-Based Charities
Senior Citizens
Climate Change
Family Services
Education
Environmental Protection
Immigration
Veterans
Gun Control
Homelessness
Farm Aid
Cancer Care
Hunger Relief
Women & Girls
Medical Research

Once you've circled the causes that most resonate with you, **ask yourself these five questions** to figure out your focus and approach:

1. What do I love about this cause?

Why does it move me? Get comfortable talking about this issue, cause, or organization and why it matters to you. Sharing your perspective and passion with others is the simplest way to raise awareness on a grassroots level.

2. Is this something I prefer to take on alone, or is it better with friends involved?

If you want to fly solo, move on to question 3. If you want to involve friends, choose your squad and organize a group chat to talk about the issue and the different ways you could get involved. Remember, **#powerinnumbers**.

3. Do I feel safe and comfortable volunteering with the organization in person?

If so, talk to your parents, reach out to the charity, and see how you can get involved directly. Many orgs offer volunteer hours on the weekends or after school. This is also a great way to meet new people: friends and mentors! If not, move to question 4.

4. Could I be effective in raising awareness at my school (drives, flyers) or through local youth clubs (donation projects, badge goals)?

If so, talk to trusted teachers, coaches, or community leaders about the best way to do this.

5. Could I also raise awareness online (with blogging, email blasts, or social media campaigns)?

If so, talk to your parents about the smartest, safest way to do this, and get posting! *Bonus round:* Pick an organization you want to highlight, and every day for a week create a post that raises awareness for the good that they do. Ask your friends to share your posts, and see how many impressions you can generate in a week. DM the charity to let them know your plan so they can give you credit and leverage your work!

Any one of these approaches can have an impact. A few done together can make a real difference. **Not an adorable one—a powerful one.**

"EMBRACE YOUR OWN VOICE. THEN RECOGNIZE THE SHEER POWER OF IT. THINK ABOUT WHAT MAKES YOU ANGRY OR MAKES YOU CRY . . . THEN USE YOUR VOICE TO DO SOMETHING ABOUT IT."

—DEBRA MESSING, ACTOR AND ACTIVIST

It Only Takes Small Steps

After wondering, *What can I do?* you might start to wonder, *Is it enough?*

It's a valid concern. The minute we dive more than two inches into an issue like clean water or teen refugees, we see how deep the problem really goes. It can suddenly seem insurmountable, and any effort we throw in that direction can seem like—*yep, this is happening*—a tiny drop in the bucket.

But, girls, don't let that immobilize you. Because it's enough to just *start*.

A small step.

A seed from which more action can grow.

It all counts.

The world's problems are big—this is true. But what is also true is that the world's past problems have been solved in small steps by regular people. *Like you.*

The changemakers of history didn't start as heroes. They took small steps to solve giant problems and encouraged others to join them along the way. And that is exactly what you can do too.

Examples, please. On it.

Let's say you start small with a school-supply drive for an underserved school in your area. Explain the idea and get other students excited to donate. Then, as your next small step, see if the local stationary or hardware store will chip in some supplies or match your donations. Then, take the step to see if an even larger chain will let you put a donation bin by the front door ("Buy a backpack, leave a backpack"). A next step could be seeing if other schools in your district or a community youth group wants to join in your efforts. Maybe they could fill the backpacks. And yet another small step might be attracting the attention of a student newspaper with your clever #DoUHaveAPencil campaign (because you took the step to give it a name and a hashtag) and a local TV station picks it up. The idea spreads. Getting the idea?

Your work doesn't have to wind up on TV. But a good idea that starts small can be scalable. **And even if it stays small, it's still enough.**

As you approach new community service projects, girls, look first for those who need you. Then do what you can and express thanks for every blessing you possess and can extend to others.

Think big. Start small. Take that first step.

Ê-Interview with Powerhouse Teen Taylor Richardson, a.k.a.

@astronautstarbright

Love reading about girls your age changing the world? We do too. Meet **Taylor Richardson**, aspiring astronaut, STEM advocate, philanthropist, and the Oprah-recognized force behind GoFundMe campaigns bringing thousands of girls to movies like *Captain Marvel*, *A Wrinkle in Time*, and *Hidden Figures*. We interviewed Taylor after one of her early film initiatives, and here's what she told us!

Ê: *Why do you think it's so important for girls to see* A Wrinkle in Time, *and what do you think is the most important lesson in the movie and others like it?*

TR: This importance is very simple: representation matters, and girls, especially those of color, need to see what they can be. This movie shows how girls can embrace their flaws and use them for good. I think the most important lesson in this movie is learning to love and accept your true self and owning it!

Ê: *Girls our age sometimes think they are too young to have an impact on the world around them. What would you say to motivated middle school girls who don't want to wait but want to change the world . . . today?*

TR: I say to those girls: Do it! If you have ideas and ways to make this world better, then make your voice heard and be the change you want to see in the world! It's that simple. As my idol Dr. Mae Jemison would say, "Never be limited by others' limited imaginations!"

> "Success means nothing if it is achieved through selfish actions. Help others in the way you would want to be helped if you were in their situation. Provide resources, volunteer your time, and use your intellect to benefit everyone around you, only then will you be truly successful!"
>
> —*Lily I., Être Board member, age seventeen*

Next Gen Giving: Ê-Interview with *inLieu* founder Kathy Terry

The phrase *in lieu* means *"instead of"* or *"in place of."* Imagine an app that would allow users to make donations *in lieu of* purchasing material gifts. Imagine that it could make donating fast, easy, and social. Imagine the "Venmo of donating." Entrepreneur **Kathy Terry** imagined exactly that, and then she went ahead and built it. With a live social feed so you can highlight your favorite charities and like or share with your friends, inLieu has the potential to change giving for the next generation. Want the inside scoop? Keep reading.

Ê: *What exactly is inLieu and why is it especially great for kids our age?*

KT: InLieu is the first app that bundles a social network with a donating platform. The idea is that you donate to your friend's favorite charity with impact instead of just giving a gift. I think it's great for kids your age because you are already so aware of the world around you and intentional about choosing sustainable brands that give back; this is just a streamlined way for you to be charitable and share the good you are doing with your network.

Ê: *We love the social side of this—the ability to celebrate friends' communions, bat mitzvahs, quinceañeras, sweet sixteens, and graduations by donating to their favorite causes! But . . . privacy. Is it safe?*

KT: Yes. Our platform allows for social interaction, but you can also make your profile private, and you can give anonymously anytime you want. We take your privacy seriously and don't share your information with anyone except the specific charity—and even then, only with your permission.

Ê: *How can it be used to raise awareness—instead of dollars—for charities we love?*

KT: InLieu is perfect for that! First, you can save and link your favorite charities to your inLieu profile, so that's the first thing your friends see (and you can change your profile charities anytime). Also, in addition to holding personal events on inLieu (donating your birthday to a charity instead of receiving gifts), we are building a public events feature where you can invite others to learn about a particular cause and fundraise.

We've collaborated with others to raise awareness for donating in honor of things like Ellen DeGeneres's birthday, SoulCycle, NYFW with *Vogue*, and the reach was wide because everyone shared it on social. **You can do this too!** Also, on the money side, there's no minimum for any donation and amounts are not disclosed. So you can give two dollars to a charity or in honor of an occasion, not disclose the amount, and still make an impact.

Ê: *What's the future of philanthropy for our generation?*

KT: Because of your generation, philanthropy will become part of our everyday lifestyle. It will be normalized and made more approachable, woven into our lives and mindsets, because your generation is so active and vocal about causes you care about. And things like inLieu will make it easy. InLieu is the future—allowing us to show our love, appreciation, gratitude, and thanks while simultaneously creating impact as a community. **The world will be ready because** YOU **guys are ready.**

"Girls have become conditioned to share the superficial on social media—funny memes or photoshopped selfies or carefully curated party shots. It would be a game-changer if you instead posted shout-outs for friends who did something substantive, whether they hustled during a softball game, or successfully challenged an unfair school policy, or reached a meaningful personal goal. Your friends would reciprocate, and over time everyone would recognize that loyalty and tenacity matter far more than popularity or appearance."

—*Phyllis L. Fagell, LCPC, school counselor at Sheridan School, frequent contributor to the* Washington Post, *and author of* Middle School Matters

"I am lucky. Very lucky. I have healthy food to eat, a roof over my head, and clothing to keep me warm. I have a supportive and loving family who is always there for me. That's why being charitable is important to me. It is significant to give back to other people. Not only are you doing a good deed, it can make you feel good about yourself. There are so many ways to be charitable. You could donate food and clothing, raise money for a charity by participating in a fundraising event, or help kids in the world who are struggling. Never take anything for granted and always pay it forward."

—*Charley L., Être Board member, age ten*

Swipe Up: How 2 Use Your Social Media Powers 4 Good

Trending: Mean girls are out. Girls with *meaning* are in.

We are ushering in a new day of young activism in which teens are teaming up, marching forward, and speaking truth to power. And girls, in particular, have been leading the way—so, girls, these words are for you. Your aunts might be knitting the hats, but it's your words on signs or at microphones around the world that are bringing us to our feet.

But what if you aren't yet ready for the mic? We see you, nodding quietly in the back, pulling your ponytail into a thin, twirly mustache across your face. Eyes wistful as you watch girls your age challenge lawmakers on TV and give speeches that go viral.

Those girls look powerful. Fearless. Engaged.

That will never be me, you think. *I want to be involved, but that will never be me.*

Hold the phone.

Maybe, just maybe, your phone is the perfect way for you to get involved at your own pace. A way to dip a toe in the water carefully, and thoughtfully make your way toward activism. **A way to use your social media powers for good.**

We know social media gets a bad rap. *Especially* for middle schoolers. It's called out as a breeding ground for bullying. A haven for the haters. The mean girls' mainstay. This can all be true. But, when used with supervision and for good, social can also be the first place a girl makes her voice heard. And that's pretty amazing. Here's how.

Think a political candidate said something worthwhile? *Give it a like.*

Read something informative you think others would enjoy? *Retweet it.*

Disagree with words or a perspective? *Comment, respectfully.*

These are small ways that you can choose your causes and your issues and then speak up, entering the conversation when and where you choose. Bonus: You can decide to step out anytime.

Or you can decide to do more.

Once you pick your issue, check out others making strides toward that goal. Choose an organization, flex those social media fingers, and get to work.

Could you give us some examples? Got it.

- Start liking and commenting on their posts. Share their posts with your squad to spread the word.

- Pay attention to cause-awareness days (like National Rescue Dog Day, International Literacy Day, World Autism Awareness Day), and create your own posts. Be sure to use the associated hashtags as well as any you create on your own. Or find an initiative just starting up (remember the athletes in chapter 5?), and join them as they make a difference.

- Create a weeklong social media campaign, posting new pics and info every day about your charity. Great graphics and a clever hashtag go a long way. Tag the lucky charity so they can leverage your work and give you some props!

In doing any of this, you'll be saying a lot.

From the comfort of your own phone, you'll be taking a stand and speaking up about something that matters to you. Engaging with a larger community about a shared interest.

Girls, you don't have to march to make a difference. At least not yet.

You can make posts instead of posters, and trade the mic for a like.

Your message will be read, and your voice *will* be heard.

Ê-NOTE: Now, some responses to your posts may be tinged with negativity. Some comments may be snarky or downright mean. *Deep breath.* Think of this as good practice for when you give a speech someday or speak first in a meeting. There will always be an opposing perspective. First, find the message behind the comment and try to see what they're really saying. If it's just empty venom, ignore it. *Deep breath again.* But if there's a point hidden in there, try to understand it. No need to respond or elevate the fight (and if things get super unpleasant, that's what social media blocking is for), but always try to listen to what may be underlying the opposition.

Because at the end of all of this, you are not the mean girl.

YOU are the girl with meaning.

#BeCharitable
IN TEN WORDS OR LESS:

START SMALL.
GIVE BIG.
IT MEANS
EVERYTHING.

CHAPTER EIGHT

#BeBrave

Close your eyes and think about the last time you were brave. We're talking fists-clenched, chin-uplifted, heart-racing brave. Maybe it was at the top of a mountain, staring down a too-steep ski slope. Maybe it was at the bottom of some basement stairs, knowing it was time to leave a party early. Or maybe it was just a quick instant in the hall, standing up for yourself. You knew it when you felt it, though. That little shot of adrenaline that said, *I've got this*.

That's the surprising thing about bravery. It shows up when you need it. It happens in the moments before a quiz, the minute you take the mic, after a slow breath in the batter's box. *And here's the secret*—bravery is always there, in your back pocket, within your reach. So reach.

This chapter reminds you to #BeBrave—brave enough to both mess up and succeed—and highlights some especially brave BFFs to keep you inspired.

> "Brave girls are the ones people want to hire. The ones they want to coach. To work for and to vote for. Because brave girls lead."
>
> —*Être*

Try Out.
Stress Less.

I want to try out, but everyone else has been playing longer.

I can't audition for stuff in front of other people.

What if I raise my hand but I'm wrong?

What if they laugh?

Two words: Stress less.

OK, three: Stress way less.

A big part of being brave is being able to step out of your comfort zone and into the unknown. That place where you might not make the team or sing pitch-perfect or nail the right answer. You might even fail in a big, spectacular way.

But at least you were brave enough to try.

Girls, that's courage.

And it's the only path to success.

One of our favorite role models, **Reshma Saujani**, talks in her book *Brave, Not Perfect* (find it in chapter 10) about a dream she had at age thirteen about running for public office. Then, with no background in politics but armed with a fervent desire to make the world better, she ran for US Congress at age thirty-three. And bravely lost. In her own words, "When I ran for public office at the age of thirty-three, it was the first time in my entire adult life that I had done something truly brave."

What happened next? She took an issue she'd discovered on the campaign trail—the tech gender gap in classrooms—and founded Girls Who Code. Yep, the awesome nonprofit that now reaches almost ninety thousand girls in all fifty states.

She was brave enough to try . . . and fail . . . and then try something entirely new.

This can be you.

Why not take a step toward something you've always wanted to try? It can be a small step—like auditioning for a supporting part in the school musical before trying out for the lead, or running for treasurer before class president—but be brave enough to try.

What if I don't get it?

We repeat: Stress. Less.

So you trip on your way to the goal. So you hiccup through your song. Like, loud, echoing hiccups. So they laugh.

If you fail, in addition to toning your bravery muscles, two other important things will happen:

1. You will learn stuff through the failure.

You will talk to people and ask *What happened? What could I have done differently?* And the most important question: *How should I gear up for next time?* These lessons will stick with you.

2. You will know you can survive failure.

Once you fail, you'll realize you can live through it. And that it's *not that bad.* Knowing you can survive an epic fail will make you more confident next time, and you'll always remember you were brave enough to put yourself out there. This makes you untouchable.

Bravery like this comes from tuning out your own negative thoughts (the "obnoxious roommate in your head," as another Être role model **Arianna Huffington** refers to them) and worrying less.

Attempting more.

Being willing to risk failure to reach your goal.

We can't promise that you won't fail. But we can 100 percent guarantee you won't know until you are brave enough to try.

So—stress less. Try out. See what happens.

"Obstacles are opportunities . . . you need to develop resilience and embrace them. Not everything will be easy, so dig deeper and work harder when things become difficult."

—*Claudia Chan, founder of S.H.E. Summit, author of* This Is How We Rise, *host of the* How We Rise *leadership podcast*

"I WANT EVERY SINGLE ONE OF US WHO HAVE LIVED AT THE MERCY OF OUR PERFECT-GIRL TRAINING TO KNOW THAT NO FAILURE WILL BREAK YOU. WILL YOU MAKE MISTAKES, MAYBE EVEN FAIL? ABSOLUTELY. WILL IT BREAK YOU? NO WAY, SISTER. NO MISTAKE OR SETBACK WILL

TAKE YOU DOWN ONCE YOU BECOME A DIE-HARD MEMBER OF TEAM BRAVE. EVERY SETBACK IS JUST ANOTHER CHANCE TO FURTHER STRENGTHEN THOSE FIERCE BRAVERY MUSCLES YOU'RE BUILDING BY GETTING BACK UP AND TRYING AGAIN."

—RESHMA SAUJANI, FOUNDER AND CEO OF GIRLS WHO CODE, NEW YORK TIMES BESTSELLING AUTHOR OF BRAVE, NOT PERFECT

Stressing Less Doesn't Mean Thinking Less

An important thing to add here is that while you're busy not caring *at all* about the snarky comments you heard after you raised your hand in French class and answered in Spanish (hey, at least you raised your hand), stressing less doesn't mean making unsafe or unwise choices.

It doesn't mean *thinking* less.

Any brave choice should still be smart. Thoughtful. Considered.

Risk-takers still rehearse, and sounding boards exist for a reason.

The point is before you take a running leap off the high dive, make sure there's water in the pool. Make sure the risk you want to take is safe and smart and that if you need a parental thumbs-up or sign-off, you have it.

Then, by all means, have at it. Go for gold.

Gather up that courage and strive for what you want.

But just like having courage doesn't guarantee success, being brave doesn't mean being reckless.

Keep your head about you and your goals in sight. Check the water level. Then, dive in.

"Being a brave girl builds your brain, your backbone, and brings out your true beauty. The more you tell the truth about how you feel, believe in your own capabilities, and respect others, the braver you become."

—*Nell Merlino, creator of Take Our Daughters to Work Day with the Ms. Foundation for Women, founder of Count Me In for Women's Economic Independence; Make Mine a Million $ Business; and Born Worthy*

Fail Bravely / Succeed Bravely

So we've talked about being brave and failing bravely. Important stuff, because so many success stories you've grown up with started out with failures. We're talking public, *tray-goes-flying-in-the-cafeteria, bad-spaghetti-everywhere* failures. For example, did you know that J. K. Rowling's first Harry Potter manuscript was rejected by twelve different publishers before finally being accepted? And did you know that first lady and rockstar lawyer Michelle Obama failed the bar exam the first time she took it? Yep, these happened along with many more. Famous women you know have failed famously.

But there is an important lesson here. These women went on to bravely succeed, and then **they were unafraid to celebrate their successes**. Never sheepish about reversing failure, never underplaying the talent or grit that brought them to the top, they were brave enough to *own* their ultimate success—even if they failed before.

This is key: Be brave enough to celebrate success.

It's not bragging. Not even a #humblebrag. It's legit.

We're talking about honoring your own success so you can leverage it into something bigger. Your next success.

For example, it's great to get your short story published in the school magazine. Worthy of praise and pride. But if you don't show it to anyone or share that news, how will a local paper or an online publishing portal see it? How will you gain more confidence and write about broader topics? How will you launch the young writer that's waiting inside you?

It's the same with your art. How will a teen gallery or an after-school art club see your talent if every piece you paint stays on your fridge? Or on your phone? Be brave enough to share your work and celebrate that first success, because it might lead to something bigger.

It feels like bragging, we know. But being confident enough to share your accomplishments is a good thing. Being determined enough to roll one success into another isn't conceited; it's goal oriented. You're building on your own hard work. **If it's done with grace, it's more brave than brag.** And you're showing younger girls that, just as it's OK to cheer others' successes, it's OK to believe in your own.

Failing bravely is, without question, a skill you want to develop. But succeeding courageously and unapologetically is also vital to a lifetime of growth—and will ensure you get the credit you deserve.

It's a kind of empowerment. So add this to your list of how to #BeBrave:

Be brave enough to celebrate success.

"Don't shy away from or dismiss compliments by attributing your success to external factors. Accept your success and be kind to yourself. Own it! When you feel undeserving, go back and review previous accomplishments or positive feedback. Recount the people you made a difference for. This will help assure you that nobody belongs here more than you do. No one is telling you to be ostentatious, but downplaying your success will help no one."

—*Hira Ali, CEO of Advancing Your Potential, and Revitalize and Rise, bestselling author of* Her Way to the Top

"WE ALL HAVE A PURPOSE AND WHILE WE MAY NOT KNOW WHAT IT IS NOW, WITH HARD WORK, BRAVERY, AND TIME, WE WILL DISCOVER WHAT WAS ONCE UNCLEAR. OUR PURPOSE."

—*Olivia R., Être Board member, age sixteen*

"There's an enormous difference between doing what society expects of you versus 'finding brave' and doing the scary thing you expect of yourself. *Make yourself proud.*"

—Kathy Caprino, career and leadership coach, founder/president of Ellia Communications and author of Breakdown, Breakthrough

"#BeBrave so that you can #BeConnected. Bravery is being able to take initiative and lead others while also being able to recognize when you need help yourself. It takes courage to ask for help, but with a strong support system such as the on-campus mentorship that Club Être provides, help is easy to find!"

—Alessandra P., Être Board member, age seventeen

"ROLE MODELS ARE IMPORTANT BECAUSE IF THEY CAN BE BRAVE, YOU CAN BE BRAVE."

—JEWEL B., ÊTRE BOARD MEMBER, AGE NINE

Be Brave Enough to Take a Breath

It takes another kind of courage to catch your breath.

Lots of talk in this chapter about brave girls. Strong girls. A generation of fearless young women ready for any challenge. That's all well and good, but, girls, we want to mention one last type of courage that you should be cultivating. When everyone around you is racing from class to practice, from piano to test prep, it's too easy to fall in line and just run with the pack. To keep the pace no matter what. But wise women who have raced in that pack want to whisper some secret advice to you:

Hit pause. Press mute. Be brave enough to breathe.

BE THE GIRL *with* UNAPOLOGETIC AMBITION

It's hard to say no to things—we get it. And it's especially hard to say no to things that are designed to be good for you: one more travel team, one extra performance. After all, you're being bombarded with messages telling you to do more. Accomplish more. Strive for more. But, girls . . . more doesn't always mean better.

And striving isn't always thriving.

It takes true self-awareness to know when to pursue something relentlessly and when to simply put it down. Lucky for you, *middle school is the ideal time* to develop that skill and, in fact, you're doing it already! When you jumped off that endless group text because you *had* to get some sleep—that was a brave move. Sleep matters, and the drama will still be there in the morning. When you put the final touches on your art project and declared it done—that was an example of listening to yourself and knowing when to stop.

It gets harder when the grown-ups in your life are the ones pushing you to do more. When teachers, coaches, and parents are encouraging you to stretch and accomplish more, it's worth listening with an open mind. After all, they know you and they've walked this path already. Maybe you *would* be less bored if you took the advanced math class. Perhaps club soccer *will* raise your game. It's possible the band *does* need someone to play a third tambourine. (OK, no. Just . . . no.)

The point is to listen well and then to look within. Ask yourself: Which activities are most important to me? What clubs do I look forward to all day? What would my week be incomplete without? Maybe that's a small list or maybe it's a whole page. But the advantage to prioritizing your crazy schedule is twofold: it helps you decide what you seriously cannot give up, and it allows you to disengage from the extras crowding your life. If you love your sport, we beg you to stay with it (see chapter 5 for more of our sideline cheering), but maybe one of the nine committees you joined has to go. It's OK to regroup. Prioritize. Breathe.

It affords you a chance *to be*.

Because, girls, no matter what, at the end of the day, you need a bit of peace. A moment to rest and reflect. Some space to quietly grow. And while we know it takes courage to face down those middle school halls every day, your bravest moments may just come from insisting on a chance to pause and catch your breath.

Original version published on Thrive Global

"Regardless of what you're doing, whether it be writing, playing, singing, experimenting, or just being, know that only you are in charge of yourself. Only you know what's best for you, and only you know what your possibilities are. You can pull yourself back up to standing and keep going because you have the tools in order to accomplish that. One person can hold an insane amount of power, so use that. And don't let anyone take it away from you."

—*Ava D., Être Board member, age seventeen*

#BeBrave
IN TEN WORDS OR LESS:

BE BRAVE ENOUGH TO FAIL, SUCCEED, AND BREATHE.

CHAPTER NINE

#BeHappy

> "Be the girl whose happiness comes from options she explores, not the opinion of others."
>
> —*Être*

Find the things that bring you joy. Then share them. Express your art. Join a team. Sing your lungs out. Keep what makes you smile close at hand. Happy up.

Seriously, did you just tell us to happy up? Yep, and here's what we mean. By middle school you know what makes you happy. You do. Whether it's your favorite class, sport, or volunteer job (*psst . . .* head to the #BeSmart, #BeStrong, or #BeCharitable chapters for more on any of those), or you are magic with a paintbrush, a video camera, or a microphone, you know what truly brings you joy. The big question is how do you keep at it, pursue it, expand it, and turn it into something larger that you can carry with you through middle school, high school, and . . . well, the rest of your life?

Think of this chapter as a magnifying glass or the zoom feature on your phone. It will help you dive deeper into the activities that make you authentically happy and springboard them into full-fledged passions. Some people will tell you that this is important as you look toward high school and college, for that "spike" everyone's talking about—the thing that differentiates you from the rest of the pack. They're not wrong, but we think you should take a bigger view. This isn't about college. This is important for your happiness right now. This is important for your happiness and fulfillment years from now.

Now that's a reason to happy up.

"YOU ARE NOT THE NUMBER OF LIKES ON YOUR INSTA ACCOUNT. YOU ARE NOT THE NUMBER OF VIEWS ON YOUR YOUTUBE CHANNEL. YOU ARE SO MUCH MORE THAN THAT. REMEMBER IT."

—ARIANNA HUFFINGTON, FOUNDER AND CEO OF THRIVE GLOBAL, AUTHOR OF THE SLEEP REVOLUTION AND THRIVE

What Makes You So Happy Your Shoes Shoot Off?

OK, you thought there would be no homework here. No lists to fill out, no worksheets. We know. But making a list here is helpful, so let's compromise: just make it in your head.

Think about what you would choose to do if you had a completely open Saturday. We mean a totally blank day. Stay in bed and surf Netflix? *Fine.* Call your friends and take over someone's basement or kitchen? *Got it.* Play music, cuddle puppies, paint, dance, skate, throw a ball, do yoga or karate in the garage, make slime, read? *Perfect.* Think of what makes you happier than anything else and how you would choose to spend a bunch of free hours if it didn't take away from anything else on your to-do list.

Maybe your list has ten things. Maybe it has two. Whatever is on that list is not the endgame; it's a starting point.

Anything that makes you so happy that you would put it first on your empty-Saturday game plan is worth making time for. And it doesn't need to involve anyone else to be worth doing. If painting is your thing and no one else is waving a brush to join, paint anyway. Put your headphones on, find a bright corner or a sunny spot outside, and get your art on.

The opposite can be true too. Maybe your happy thing would actually be way more fun with a squad. Call some friends and get them on board. And if none of your friends share this particular interest, that's OK too! Just because you don't know anyone your age who loves chess doesn't mean they're not out there. A quick search of local chess clubs or parks with official play might just up your happy game and be an unexpected way to meet new friends.

The thing to keep in mind is that whatever makes you happy—authentically, my-shoes-might-shoot-off-I'm-so-giddy kind of happy—is worth your time. Move it to the forefront of your Saturday, and then see if you can work it in during the week. We know how busy (*looks around,* overscheduled, *who said that?*) you are. Seriously, who has time to add a single other activity?

Um, you do.

Because the thing that makes you smile uncontrollably and jump out of bed on a Saturday is a thing to stick with. And pursue.

So, keep thinking about it. What makes you absurdly happy? How can you do more of it? Make some room for that kind of happy. Do it now and for the rest of your life.

Quick Ways to Happiness

At Être, we surveyed our network of middle and high school girls for the things that are guaranteed to make them smile. Here are just a few! If you're in need of a happiness pick-me-up, try some of these. We bet they'll make you :) too.

> **Bad karaoke**
> *Beaches*
> **Blank canvases**
> **Campfires**
> Championships
> *Coachella*
> Convertibles
> **Cool aunts**
> Cupcakes
> *Dry shampoo*
> Fireworks
> ***First snow***
> **Flip-flops**

> **Good causes**
> ***Green smoothies***
> Live comedy
> *Long naps*
> **Loud friends**
> **Marshmallow Peeps (don't judge)**
> **More sleep**
> Netflix
> *New books*
> **Olympic Games**
> **Photo booths**
> **Pretzel M&M's**
> *Roller coasters*
> Scoring goals
> **Shared playlists**
> *Spring break*
> **TV awards shows**
> ***White T-shirts***
> Worn sneakers
> **Writing in journals**

"Take risks. Try new things. Meet new people. #BeHappy doing what you love."

—*Darby L., Être Board member, age fourteen*

The Happy You Haven't Found Yet

But what if I haven't found my favorite hobby yet? What if I don't have four travel teams, a personal art website, or my own YouTube channel? Hello, I'm eleven. How do I pursue my happy if it hasn't shown up yet?

Great point.

The short answer is . . . try a bunch of new things. And be ready to be bad at some of them. Because when we say "new things," we mean thinking way out of the box! If you're not a fan of typical team sports, one more run at JV volleyball might not rock your world. But what about archery (think *Brave*, *The Hunger Games*, Geena Davis), flag football (check out what Jen Welter, the first female NFL coach,

is doing in chapter 5), or Ultimate Frisbee (no equipment required, found on college campuses everywhere, and seriously . . . anyone can play this) as alternatives? Yeah, you might accidentally land an arrow on a roof or sail a Frisbee through a math class, but you might be happy doing it!

Similarly, if you think you like art but are mortified to display your paintings when the school art show rolls around, try a different type of art! Photography, digital art, or mixed media collaging might showcase your artistic vision in a fresh new way, using tools easily found on your phone or the school computer. Or try a different outlet for your art. Local and regional art shows are often delighted to add student art to their exhibitions, and displaying your work to strangers is sometimes easier than to peers.

If choir is a *thanks but hard no* for you, but you make amazing mash-ups, what about songwriting, music mixing, or DJ classes? You are so over the school newspaper but still want to publish? Investigate teen-only magazines or writing platforms where you can share your thoughts via poetry, short stories, or journalistic reporting. The lists are endless, the resources plentiful, and your options sky-wide. All it takes is a little courage, a willingness to fail, and the certitude that you will find *your thing*.

Ê-NOTE: This thing is for *you*. It's not for future applications or internships. It's not to impress others. It's not for your parents. It's for your own happiness. Find a passion and set it on fire.

"WHEN YOU TRULY WANT SOMETHING, THE ENTIRE UNIVERSE CONSPIRES IN HELPING YOU TO ACHIEVE IT."

—Komal Singh, Engineering Program Manager at Google and creator of STEM bestseller Ara the Star Engineer *(paraphrasing Paulo Coelho in* The Alchemist*)*

"I pursue my passion of dance by dancing six days a week! When I dance, I can let go of all my troubles! Dancing helps me #BeHappy!"

—Cheyenne H., Être Board member, age fifteen

"Be autonomous. Don't be afraid to fail, and don't let others tell you what should make you happy. Be who you are and pursue your passion. Do things that make you truly happy. Always."

—*Gabriella R., Être Board member, age seventeen*

"I AM WHAT I WANT TO BE WHEN I GROW UP, BECAUSE IT'S NEVER TOO EARLY TO PURSUE THE THINGS YOU ARE PASSIONATE ABOUT. I AM AN ARTIST."

—*Chloé B., Être Board member, age thirteen*

Springboard Your Passions: Contests, Spotlights, Showcases You Should Know About

When middle and high school Être girls asked for *specific* ways to springboard their interests, we went looking. Here are a few we found helpful. There are zillions of others, though, and we're happy to help find the one that's exactly right for you! Email us at info@etregirls.com and we'll shoot you suggestions tailored for you. Not even kidding.

Congressional Award: If you're up for a challenge, this is a great way to get more involved with something you already enjoy . . . or try something brand new! You can register anytime after you turn thirteen. The idea is to work toward new goals you set for yourself (as opposed to being honored for past achievements) in four areas: *public service, personal development, physical fitness, and expedition/exploration*. This award is nonpartisan, noncompetitive, and *all* about diving deeper into what makes you happy!

Girls Write Now: Does writing make you happy? Wish you had a personal mentor for high-level guidance? Girls Write Now pairs a diverse population of girls (90 percent girls of color, 70 percent immigrant or first generation, 25 percent LGBT/nonconforming, and 90 percent high need) with professional female writers to reach their writing goals. This makes us all kinds of happy.

International Songwriting Competition: Feeling happy at the top of your lungs? Want to have your original songs heard in a professional arena? This songwriting competition is open to both amateurs and professionals of any age (someone else can sing it, you don't have to), and bonus feature: entrants must be eighteen *or younger* to enter the Teen category! Categories include Country, EDM, Music Video, Pop/Top 40, R&B/Hip-Hop, Rock, Teen, and more. Happy up to a beat, people.

BE THE GIRL GOING PLACES

Scholastic Art & Writing Awards:
This is a major contest that can spring-board your art and writing across twenty-nine different categories to major acclaim. Teens in grades 7–12 (ages thirteen and up) are eligible, you can win at the regional or national level *(oh, gold medal winners are honored at Carnegie Hall, NBD)*, and winning can result in scholarships and your work being exhibited or published in a big way. Stop smiling, we dare you.

Teen Ink: A magazine, book series, and website created *by* teens *for* teens, *Teen Ink* offers girls like you the chance to publish original poetry, fiction, art, photography, and videos on issues affecting you and your generation. This is a great way to broaden your audience *(hint:* their print magazine reaches 300,000 readers every month, and even more via their website) and express your creativity.

"I worked with Être to receive my Girl Scout Gold Award because being happy, strong, and true to yourself are all characteristics that help kids develop confidence, reduce anxiety, and find real joy in life."

—*Amanda P., Être Board member, age sixteen*

Other Ways 2 Start

Let's say that you're somewhere in between making a list in your head and entering an international contest. What are some other low-key but high-impact ways of finding your happy? We're big fans of exploring everything from books to online videos and TED talks for inspiration. Here are a few ideas to investigate:

Books and manuals: Yep, we're starting old-school. Take a walk to the library or your local bookstore and *ask*. Then spend time in the stacks perusing different topics. If you're surfing on Amazon, *search*. Stay age appropriate and then craft searches

that reflect your latest hobby, activity, or interest. Books can be teachers and are the start of . . . well, everything.

IRL classes: We know you have enough school on your plate, but every now and then a fun weekend class is worthwhile. Maybe a free week-long class over the summer? Learning in person has advantages, and new teachers, *you guessed it,* can become future mentors.

Online classes: Nothing in person available? No worries, hop online. Same advice: stay age appropriate (maybe now's a good time to grab an older sibling or parent to help you look). Online classes at the middle or high school level can often pick up where your regular classrooms stop, and encourage you to explore new subjects. You might even find a class on happiness!

TED talks: *Ohhhh,* Être girls love TED talks! Quick, packed with info, and usually featuring lively presenters, TED talks are a terrific way to learn about new things. Don't miss their playlists of talks by brilliant kids and teens, their TED-Ed library of lessons, and assorted TEDx talks with local speakers.

YouTube tutorials: YouTube is a great learn-to-do-this resource for anything from DIY crafts to geometry. Want to start a sneaker-decorating business or learn to play the guitar? YouTube can help. But, like anything on your phone, keep your eyes open and your wits about you. Listen to that smart girl voice in your head, whether it whispers *bad idea* or *cutest sneakers ever,* and #BeSmart.

Ê–NOTE: A word about phones: They are not the source of *all* information.

Nor are they the source of all evil. Put another way, they shouldn't be your first and only go-to for anything. Yes, your access to resources, mentors, and global connections can be fueled at the touch of a button. But your experiences and adventures, the things that put purpose and meaning behind your networks, are best done without a phone in your hand. It's not just that certain research suggests a connection between screen time and youth depression and anxiety. It's that **being present in the moment can lead to greater happiness**.

#TRUTH: Some things are just more fun without a phone.

"#BeHappy—I think authenticity is one of the most important things for people today. By being genuine and transparent, there is no comparison between you and anyone else, because you are original."

—Eden O., Être Board member, age seventeen

Pocket. That. Phone.

Pocket the *what*? Sorry, did you say *put it down*? Yeah, we did. Your happiness may depend on it.

Sure, the world is on your phone. Your homework, your friends, that weirdest filter *ever* that you cannot stop playing with . . . we understand. And adults are just as guilty. Your Spanish teacher checks his phone obsessively during breaks. Your coach's phone might be permanently attached to her ear. And your parents email during dinner. All. During. Dinner. But maybe you—the girl with her finger on the pulse of every trend—can set the example.

#PocketThatPhone.

After all, you are the true professionals here. You can text while your phone is actually in your pocket—we've seen you do it. So you know what? Leave it there. Just for a few minutes. Try an hour. Graduate to a whole meal. The adults around you are literally walking into walls—*yeah, it happened once*—because they can't put down their phones. It's time to enlighten them. Like it or not, you are the age demographic that marketers use to determine what's in each season. Maybe the hot new thing will be . . . um, eye contact.

Teach us how to unplug.

Truth be told, we only got plugged in because of you. We joined Facebook to keep tabs on our kids and see our friends' families more often . . . and now you're not even there. We made Instagram accounts because you said it was cool . . . now we can't find you in the filters. We can't keep up or keep our focus . . . and we did this all for you. So you have to help us.

Seriously, rescue us.

We can't stay uberengaged on all fronts like this, and frankly neither can you. You know how much better you feel on the soccer field or out on the ice. You recognize the sheer bliss of diving through ocean waves or singing your lungs out onstage. Do you know what's nowhere to be found when you feel like that? Rhymes with *drone*.

We know there is undeniable joy in connecting with others. Bringing you into the world taught us that above all else. But there is equal joy to be found in pursuing your passions and seeing just how high you can leap untethered. Because those are the moments when unbridled happiness bursts through and you run your hands through your hair, amazed that one moment could contain so much joy. Again, hard to do with something else in your hand.

So, pocket the phone—just now and then. **Things that are fundamentally gratifying take focus.** Measured breath. Two hands outstretched for balance. You can pick it up later and share all the cool stuff you did in your own unique, artistic way. But what you post—the waves you surfed, the basket you made, the magic you splashed across that canvas—let all of that happen with your phone somewhere else. Set a good example for the phone-obsessed grown-ups in your life. We'll thank you for it, repeatedly.

Original version published on Thrive Global

"I believe it is wonderful to be unique as you are. We all have a purpose here, so explore your passions. You got this!"

—Nayley G., Être Board member, age seventeen

"Even though my work focuses on balance for women, so much of what I've gleaned can apply to girls too because you all also have so much on your plates between school, homework, friends, activities, family, et cetera. It's a whole lot to manage! Just remember that no one is doing it all perfectly. It may look that way (especially on Snapchat and Instagram), but everyone has the same amount of hours in the day. Figure out how to allocate your hours so you are being your most authentic and then embrace that, do that, be that person. Because only when you are being your most authentic and true to yourself and your own priorities (not the priorities of other girls who have different strengths and weaknesses than you, different family/health/financial situations, et cetera) will you soar to reach the beautiful potential that is inside you!"

—*Susie Orman Schnall, author of* The Subway Girls, The Balance Project, *and* On Grace; *creator of* The Balance Project Interviews

KEEP WHAT MAKES YOU SMILE CLOSE AT HAND. HAPPY UP.

CHAPTER TEN

#BeWellRead

As kids, we hid under the covers with flashlights to read. Now we squint in the dark at our screens. The obsession is the same. Books, and the worlds that break open with their pages, are portals to joy, reflection, and imagination. Think of your earliest heroes: They spun webs and walked through wardrobes. They traveled by covered wagon . . . or sometimes by bubble. Later, they won Quidditch bowls, defeated the Capitol, and started saying "doth" a lot. Books inform us about the past and the present while offering glimpses of the future. They spark our creativity, help us study, research, and invent. And they reward us with gripping tales of adventure and love. Most of all, they give us mentors, role models, and endless friends.

That's right . . . characters can be all these things.

Put simply, books are magic.

Part of the magic can be found in the variety of books out there, so in this last chapter we want to leave you with this: **Read. Everything.** Just as we advised in chapter 6 when we talked about news sites, read for breadth and depth. Read from unexpected sources to hear undiscovered viewpoints. Read trending titles alongside beloved classics, and exchange book recommendations between classes. Share your faves, trade copies, and be undeterred if you're the only one who loves a certain genre or series. Be the girl who reads everything and ultimately finds her own magic.

"I've never been forced to fight a bunch of kids to the death in a televised arena, but I've read *The Hunger Games*, so I know exactly how that would be. The tradition of storytelling is the closest thing that we have to a comprehensive instruction manual on how to manage the human experience. The more books you read, the better prepared you will be to tackle real life with wisdom, courage, and strength. #BeWellRead."

—ANNABEL MONAGHAN, AUTHOR OF DOES THIS VOLVO MAKE MY BUTT LOOK BIG?, A GIRL NAMED DIGIT, DOUBLE DIGIT, AND CLICK!

Ê-Reads and Recommendations

Rather than writing about all of our favorite books and everything they have meant to us, we thought we'd drop you in the middle of a virtual book club, giving you a quick look at some Être recommendations. This list, which is in no way comprehensive or exhaustive, is meant to hat tip our favorite authors and highlight titles that might not be on your shelf or screen yet. We'd love to hear about your picks, and we'll add a bunch to the list we keep updated on the site. But for now (keeping school requirements and household guidelines in mind), read everything that grabs your attention. Read to learn, relax, and laugh so hard Gatorade comes out your nose. Good book clubs are vaults—we'll never tell.

HEY, U UP? READ **EVERYTHING** ON MY SHELF . . . NEED NEW RECS ASAP! TXT ME.

Ara the Star Engineer by Komal Singh *(good for younger kids u babysit)*

Becoming by Michelle Obama

Born Just Right by Jordan Reeves and Jennifer Reeves

Brave, Not Perfect by Reshma Saujani *(high school age +)*

Crack the Code: Activities, Games, and Puzzles That Reveal the World of Coding by Sarah Hutt

Enough As She Is by Rachel Simmons

Fierce: How Competing for Myself Changed Everything by Aly Raisman *(high school age +)*

First Women: The Grace and Power of America's Modern First Ladies by Kate Andersen Brower

Geek Girl Rising by Heather Cabot and Samantha Walravens *(high school age +)*

Girl Mogul by Tiffany Pham

Girls Who Code: Learn to Code and Change the World by Reshma Saujani

I Got This by Laurie Hernandez

Ignite Your Spark by Patricia Wooster *(twelve +)*

Lights, Music, Code! (book 3 in Girls Who Code series) by Jo Whittemore

Marley Dias Gets It Done: And So Can You! by Marley Dias *(OMG we know her)*

Raise Your Hand by Alice Paul Tapper *(oh, and she's eleven . . . NBD)*

Strong Is the New Pretty: A Celebration of Girls Being Themselves by Kate T. Parker

The Confidence Code for Girls by Katty Kay and Claire Shipman

This Is How We Rise by Claudia Chan *(high school age +)*

Women In Sports: 50 Fearless Athletes Who Played to Win by Rachel Ignotofsky *(def also get Women In Science: 50 Fearless Pioneers Who Changed The World)*

NOPE, I'M OLD-SCHOOL. JUST WANT MORE CLASSIC READS . . . **ALL. OF. THEM.** SEND NAMES, PLS.

A Wrinkle in Time *(book 1 in Time Quintet series)* by Madeleine L'Engle

Anne of Green Gables *(book 1 in Anne of Green Gables series)* by L. M. Montgomery

Ella Enchanted by Gail Carson Levine

Esperanza Rising by Pam Muñoz Ryan

Frankenstein by Mary Shelley

Hattie Big Sky by Kirby Larson

Little Women by Louisa May Alcott

National Velvet by Enid Bagnold

Pride and Prejudice by Jane Austin

The Diary of a Young Girl by Anne Frank

The Joy Luck Club by Amy Tan

To Kill a Mockingbird by Harper Lee

Tuck Everlasting by Natalie Babbitt

WAIT, I FEEL IDEAS COMING ON . . . **HAND ME A JOURNAL!**

Create Your Me Movement by Patricia Wooster

I Love Science: A Journal for Self-Discovery and Big Ideas by Rachel Ignotofsky

My Rad Life Journal by Kate Schatz

Strong Is The New Pretty: A Guided Journal for Girls by Kate T. Parker

The Gutsy Girl: Escapades for Your Life of Epic Adventure by Caroline Paul

"'Think instead of react.' Author Adriana Trigiani said that at a book reading I attended, and it made me think. We are constantly receiving information through social media and the internet, and much of the information we share and receive is based on reactions. Maybe it's time we start thinking more; reading books, writing down our ideas, creating stories, taking some time to just think and reflect."

—ISABELLA M., ÊTRE BOARD MEMBER, AGE SIXTEEN

A Girl Named Digit (book 1 in Digit series) by Annabel Monaghan

A Whole New Ball Game by Sue Macy

Almost Astronauts: 13 Women Who Dared to Dream by Tanya Lee Stone

Divergent (book 1 in Divergent series) by Veronica Roth

Dot. by Randi Zuckerberg (bc ur younger sister needs heroines too)

Edge of Yesterday by Robin Stevens Payes

Game Face: What Does a Female Athlete Look Like? by Jane Gottesman

Girls Who Rocked the World: Heroines from Joan of Arc to Mother Teresa by Michelle Roehm McCann and Amelie Welden

Hidden Figures by Margot Lee Shetterly

I Am Malala by Malala Yousafzai (we wish we knew her)

I Am Unique by Jennifer Vassel

Let Me Play: The Story of Title IX by Karen Blumenthal

Rad American Women A–Z by Kate Schatz

She Persisted: 13 American Women Who Changed the World by Chelsea Clinton (also good 4 younger sibs)

Soul Surfer by Bethany Hamilton

Steps to Success: An Empowerment Guide (from Girls Above Society) by Lauren Marie Galley (so crazy, we know her too!)

Style Engineers Worldwide (series) by Kristen O. Bobst

The Hunger Games (book 1 in the Hunger Games series) by Suzanne Collins

The Other Einstein by Marie Benedict (high school age +)

Through My Eyes by Ruby Bridges

Women in Blue: 16 Brave Officers, Forensics Experts, Police Chiefs, and More by Cheryl Mullenbach

DEVOUR
CLASSICS.
DOWNLOAD
NEW RELEASES.
DISCOVER
WORLDS WITHIN
WORDS.

"THERE IS SOMETHING SPECIAL ABOUT FINDING A MENTOR WHO HAS . . . YOU KNOW, ACTUALLY *BEEN* A MIDDLE SCHOOL GIRL AND CAN RELATE TO THE HIGH-TOPS YOU'RE STANDING IN."

—ÊTRE

When asked *"Who are you?"* and *"What do you want to be?"* I think for a moment before saying anything. I don't make up a job or future profession—I think of who I want to be as a person, because that is first and most important. Plans for the future come later; what comes first is who you are and who you want to be—today and from today on.

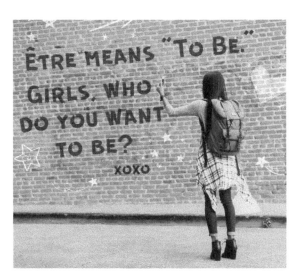

Être means *"to be,"* but what exactly is it that we all want to be? There are ten things that everyone should consider when presented with this soul-searching question, and Être explains each and every one perfectly.

#BeSmart.
Think outside the box, ask the questions nobody else thinks to ask, and learn from your mistakes.

#BeInnovative.
No idea you have will ever be too small—the world wants to see all that you have to offer.

#BeWi$e.

Know an opportunity when you see one, understand how to evaluate what you're working for, and be the girl that knows how to talk about money.

#BeConnected.

Stay close to the people you love and who inspire you, and learn as much as you can from the people you look up to.

#BeStrong.

Mental strength is just as important as physical strength, and a strong mind and values lead to a stronger, healthier you.

#BeInformed.

Be informed about what is going on around you and the world that you live in. Know how to take action, make an impact, and create change.

#BeCharitable.

Gift others with your time and talents, and help those who have a harder time helping themselves. The act of giving feels so much better than receiving.

#BeBrave.

Don't be afraid to speak up and to feel confident in who you are and what you do. Take a chance and make yourself known.

#BeHappy.

Happiness comes in many shapes and forms, so find the things that shine a little extra light into your everyday life. Do more of what you love and never forget to always express your inner self.

#BeWellRead.

Reading is the solution to expanding your mind and strengthening your brainpower in ways you may have never thought. Pick up a book that seems fascinating to you and get inspired.

Empowerment is one of the qualities so many girls forget they possess. Once you find what drives it, use it until you make yourself—and the rest of the world—know *exactly* who you are.

—*Sophia S., Être Board member, age eighteen*

A THANK-YOU NOTE
FROM MIDDLE SCHOOL GIRLS

This is our first time writing a book. And we did it all together—as the founder, I wrote a bunch of articles; luminary women shared their wisdom; and Être girls added invaluable insight. We like to give credit where it's due, and, more than that, we like to express gratitude when we owe a debt to the past. Our mothers taught us that thank-you notes are important, and they're right. Here, then, as the last article in the book, is a heartfelt thank-you note to the women who have led the way. Originally published for Women's History Month, we offer it here as a fitting ending to a book about mentorship, empowerment, and being brave enough to lead from a young age. On behalf of middle school girls everywhere, thank you.

For Those Who Led the Way

A Thank-You Note from Middle School Girls

Everywhere we look, female role models are rising. From the C-suites to the schools, from the Olympics to the Oscars, from the statehouses to the streets—we can be in no doubt of the groundswell of motivated women leading the way. Movements like #MeToo, renewed efforts on behalf of equal pay, and record numbers of women running for—and winning—elected office offer diverse new role models who are younger, louder, and more relatable to girls than perhaps ever before.

We are awed. We are energized.

And grateful middle school girls want to say thank you.

Thank you for appearing indelibly on the pages of our first history books. To the founding mothers, the early candidates, the suffragists, the abolitionists, and the freedom riders—**thank you for showing us what brazen courage looks like and what being first means.**

To the innovators we learn about in STEM classes: the physicists, the surgeons, the engineers, and the astronauts—thank you. For the inventors, the lab luminaries, the mathematicians, and the tech wizards—**thank you for sparking our imaginations and for confirming that there's no right age for a good idea.**

For the poets and the painters, the athletes and the actors, the dancers onstage, and the rockers on our playlists—thank you for using acceptance speeches for good and Olympic podiums with purpose. **Thank you for showing us that music has no gender and talent has no limit.**

For the founders and the writers, the teachers and the leaders, the CEOs, soldiers, and caregivers, the politicians, and the peacemakers—thank you for the wise words and the hard decisions. **Thank you for voting your conscience and speaking truth to power. We're standing and applauding.**

And we can't be stopped.

We'll cheer until hoarse and then whisper our thanks.

Because whether you led during our nation's earliest days or just took your first oath of office . . . whether you are a woman at the height of her career or a high school student just finding her voice . . . *you are leading today's girls.*

And we are grateful.

So, to those who led the way—in every field and at any age—we say thank you. Good manners dictate this gets said during Women's History Month, but gratitude like this bears repeating every day.

We're watching. We're listening. And we're running down the path you laid at our feet.

Original version published on Thrive Global

BE THE GIRL *who* FILLS BIG SHOES

Ê-ROCKSTARS AND Ê-RESOURCES

When Être started in 2016, We never could have imagined the organic way our network would unfold. From our first emails asking if accomplished girlfriends would talk with middle school girls about their jobs, to the text and Insta campaign that began among the girls themselves, Être's message spread whisper-style and at the grassroots level. *Have you heard* might be our favorite phrase in . . . ever.

So, in the spirit of *hey, you should know about this*, we put together a list of Être's favorite things: the luminary women and inspirational girls who gave us quotes for the book, the companies that hosted our first Lunch & Learns, and the BFFs sharing valuable resources with us online. We gave you all their info so you can follow their work and keep up with their amazingness.

OK, seriously . . . you have to meet our friends.

Ê-Rockstars in the Book

Wise women (all @Insta unless marked otherwise):

Adrianne Haslet—@adriannehaslet | #BostonStrong survivor | global advocate for amputee rights | ballroom dancer | blade runner | our hero | adriannehaslet.com

Anjali Forber-Pratt—@anjalifp84 | US paralympic medalist | PhD | assistant professor at Vanderbilt | learn about her research and *allllll* the medals at anjfp.com

Annabel Monaghan—@annabelmonaghan | author of the Digit books (*A Girl Named Digit*, *Double Digit*, and *Click!*) | series stars MIT math whiz urging girls to be their authentic selves while cracking codes | her books make us not hate algebra | annabelmonaghan.com

Arianna Huffington—@thrive founder and CEO | @HuffPost founder | author of *Thrive* and *The Sleep Revolution* | the #rolemodel who answered our email four weeks after Être launched, asked us to film a #TalkToMe video, and changed absolutely everything

Asha Castleberry—@ashacastleberry | national security expert | university professor of international politics and political economy | military combat veteran | we want to take every class she teaches

Beth Shubin Stein—@hspecialsurgery orthopedic surgeon | female athlete specialist | proof that girls can juggle a zillion balls in the air and catch them all

Cate Luzio—@bealuminary founder and CEO | super amazing banker before Luminary | building the kind of girls' clubhouses we need to run the world

Claire Shipman—@confidencecodegirls | journalist GMA, NBC, CNN (really good journalist; think Peabody, DuPont, Emmy Awards) | coauthor of *The Confidence Code for Girls* | makes us want to #captureconfidence

Claudia Chan—@shesummit founder and CEO | host of *How We Rise* leadership podcast and courses | author of *This Is How We Rise* | the kind of mentor whose words will change your life

Debra Messing—@therealdebramessing | actor and activist | inspiring every girl to find her voice, raise it, and change the world

Emily Calandrelli—@thespacegal | MIT engineer | Emmy-nominated TV science host and executive producer for #Xplorationouterspace @Fox | author of our fave Ada Lace books | thespacegal.com

Hira Ali—@advancingyou CEO | Revitalize and Rise CEO | founding director of The Career Excel For Trailblazing Women | author of *Her Way to the Top* | leading us all the way to the top

Jane Elfers—@childrensplace CEO | showing us how powerhouse CEOs get it done | believes in #kidspiration and that girls can do absolutely anything

Jayshree Seth—@3M Corporate Scientist | first ever Chief Science Advocate at 3M | holds the highest position within the technical ranks at 3M | also holds sixty-six patents and all our esteem

Jen Welter—@welter47 | first female NFL coach | founder of Grrridiron Girls | author of *Play Big* | 2X gold medalist *with* a PhD | #coachjen wants every girl to #kickglass | jenwelter.com

Jennifer Openshaw—@girlswithimpact founder and CEO | speaker, advisor, and author | girlswithimpact.com | creating #nextgen leaders ready to rule the world

Jody Rudman—lawyer extraordinaire | appeared in hundreds of non-law TV commercials | argued a case before the US Supreme Court | *Fun Fact:* One of the justices was also one of her law professors

Julia Landauer—@julialandauer | @NASCAR champion | won Skip Barber Race at age fourteen | studied science and tech at Stanford, so she also knows *why* cars go fast | julialandauer.com | keeping girls on the fast track

Kathy Caprino—@kathycaprino | Finding Brave expert | writer | speaker | leadership coach | helping tomorrow's leaders find their brave

Kathy Terry—@giveinlieu founder and CEO | redefining the way we give to charity | birthday and graduation gifts just got So. Much. Cooler.

Kellie Gerardi—@kelliegerardi | citizen scientist | astronaut candidate | Truman National Security Project Defense Council member | exploring kelliegerardi.com will blow your mind

BUILDING A NEW WORLD

Komal Singh—engineering program manager @Google | author of @arathestarengineer | STEM advocate for our very youngest Être girls

Kristy Wallace—@ellevate_ntwk CEO | host of *Ellevate* podcast: Conversations with Women Changing the Face of Business | helping women and girls elevate themselves every day

Marie Benedict—@authormariebenedict | author of *The Other Einstein, Carnegie's Maid,* and *The Only Woman in the Room* | bringing girls everywhere into the room

Marisol Castro—@marysolcastrotv | first female PA announcer @mets | first Latina PA announcer in @MLB sports league | urging girls to stay on the field and in their cleats

Maura Cunningham—@girlsrockwallstreet founder and executive director | sparking the interest of high school girls in careers in finance | gain money mentorship by following #RTSWS and #GirlsRockFinance

Michelle Waterson—@karatehottiemma | MMA fighter | former Invicta FC champion | UFC strawweight division | model, TV actress, and movie stunt star | we want her in our corner

Nancy Lieberman—retired legal legend | youngest partner ever (male or female) at the global law firm Skadden | mergers and acquisitions guru | spinal cord injury research activist

Neha Gandhi—@nehaintown | editor in chief and COO of @girlboss | also rocked the worlds of *Refinery29, Harper's Bazaar, Seventeen,* and *InStyle* | definition of a #girlboss

Nell Merlino—@nell.merlino | creator of Take Our Daughters To Work Day with the Ms. Foundation | leading girls forward since 1993 | now launching Born Worthy—you want to check it out

Phyllis Fagell—@pfagell | K–8 school counselor | @washingtonpost contributor—parenting and education | author of *Middle School Matters* | head to phyllisfagell.com for more of what matters

Reshma Saujani—@girlswhocode founder and CEO | author of *Brave, Not Perfect; Girls Who Code,* and *Women Who Don't Wait in Line* | creator of *Brave, Not Perfect* podcast | we can't wait to vote for her someday

RoriAnn Shonk—@jetblue first officer | completed first flight at fifteen years old | gave us one of Être's first inspirational quotes on #BeSmart | inspiring us ever since

Sallie Krawcheck—@Ellevest CEO and cofounder | on a mission to close the gender money gap and get more money in the hands of more women | wants every girl to ultimately #investlikeawoman

Susan Rocco—@womentowatchmedia founder | radio host spotlighting women and girls in game-changing roles | making radio seem easy and our possibilities seem limitless

Susie Orman Schnall—@susieormanschnall | author of *The Subway Girls, The Balance Project,* and *On Grace* | creator of The Balance Project Interviews | role model for every upcoming writer

Tiffany Pham—@onmogul founder and CEO | her platform reaches women and girls across 196 countries | yup, 30,470 cities | author of *Girl Mogul* and *You Are a Mogul* | we literally want *to be* her

Tracy Byrnes—@UBS financial advisor | former Fox Business anchor and host of #AlphaRising on TheStreet | author of *Break Down Your Money* | ultimate #wi$e girl

Game-changing girls (all @Insta unless marked otherwise):

Abigail Harrison—@astronautabby | @themarsgeneration founder and CEO | *Forbes* 30U30 '19 | #AskAbby STEM YouTube series | we want to tune in to everything she does

Allie Weber—@robotmakergirl (Twitter) | fourteen-year-old @MythBusters | award-winning inventor | maker | YouTube Tech-nic-Allie Speaking | *Teen Vogue* 21U21 '17 | robot @Lottie_doll | TheSTEAMSquad. org | tech-nic-allie one of our favorite teen inventors

Gitanjali Rao—@gitanjaliarao (Twitter) | @3M @DiscoveryEd #YoungScientist Challenge winner 2017 | *Forbes* 30U30 '19 | STEM advocate | making girls smarter and water cleaner every day

Ivanna Hernandez—@IvannaHernndez1 (Twitter) | sixteen-year-old aspiring astronaut, airplane pilot, and aerospace engineer | wants to be the first Latin American woman to go to Mars | TheSTEAMSquad.org | we'll go anywhere she's flying

Jordan Reeves—@jordanjustright | @bjrorg cofounder | fourteen-year-old prosthetic designer | coauthor of *Born Just Right* | Mattel collaborator | TheSTEAMSquad.org | she had us at her first glitter-shooting creation

Julie Seven Sage— @supernovastylesciencenews @7sagelabs | fifteen-year-old aspiring astrophysicist | cocreator, host, and writer of 7 Sage Labs on YouTube | TheSTEAMSquad.org | her channel rules—we can't stop watching

Morgan DiCarlo—TEDx speaker | former NASA climate researcher | ASCE and Disney Imagineering honoree | named one of America's top 10 new faces of civil engineering 2015 | if she builds it, we will come

Sammy Wolfe—fingerfirelax.com | teen inventor of a rechargeable heated lacrosse stick | changing the LAX game for players and inspiring young entrepreneurs everywhere

Sarah Cronk—@sparkleeffect founder and CEO | 2018 @worldofchildren hero award | inclusion advocate | bringing inclusion off the sidelines and under the Friday night lights

Taylor Richardson— @astronautstarbright | changemaker at first White House State of Women Summit | sixteen-year-old award-winning speaker and activist | *Teen Vogue* 21U21 | GoFundMe

hero | TheSTEAMSquad.org | we're honored to know her

Companies hosting our first Lunch & Learns (because they want more girls at the table):

Geena Davis Institute on Gender in Media—@GDIGM (Heard execs from Marvel, Sesame Workshop, If/Then, and Nat Geo discuss brand-new data about STEM roles in media)

Goldman Sachs—@goldmansachs (Visited a trading floor, had a mini-MBA course in global markets, and met everyone from analysts to MDs)

Google—@google (Floored by every engineer and exec we met and awed that they answered every question we had; we want to live in their offices)

Morgan Stanley—@morgan.stanley (Riveting panels and impactful mentors talked tech, wealth management, career paths, and diversity; oh, and our name was in their lobby lights)

NYSE—@nyse (We were everywhere: behind the scenes, in the balcony, and on the floor. Held the gavel. Hey there, Fearless Girl!)

Spotify—@spotify (Our very first Lunch & Learn—and it blew our minds. Soundstages, rooftops, brainstorming rooms, and more—it all began right here)

The Wing—@the.wing (We chatted with Nell Merlino about how she started the original Take Our Daughters to Work Day and what she's doing now with Born Worthy . . . on the first day of Women's History Month!)

Viacom—@viacom (Hung on the set of *TRL*, met ultrainspiring execs from five different departments, and talked MTV, Comedy Central, Nick, career paths, and way more)

YouTube—@youtube (Part of the Google day but a whole new experience! Saw clips filming, green rooms . . . went backstage and onstage. Coolest.)

Ê-Resources for Être Girls

Because, sharing is caring. And these orgs care like crazy.

3M
www.3m.com
Follow @3M #Lifewith3M #WonderWithUs

4GirlsTech
www.4girlstech.com
Follow teen founder @mercer.henderson

500 Women Scientists
https://500womenscientists.org
Follow @500womensci

AI4All
www.ai-4-all.org
Follow @ai4allorg

All In Together
https://aitogether.org
Follow @AllInTogether

Black Girls Code
www.blackgirlscode.com
Follow @BlackGirlsCode

Born Worthy
https://bornworthy.org
Follow their founder @Nell.Merlino

Career Girls
www.careergirls.org
Follow @career_girls

Columbia Girls in STEM
http://sps.columbia.edu/girls-in-stem
Follow @Columbia_SPS

DiscoverE
http://discovere.org
Follow @discovereorg

Discovery Education
www.discoveryeducation.com
Follow @Discoveryed

Ellevate Network
www.ellevatenetwork.com
Follow @ellevate_ntwk

Ellevest
www.ellevest.com
Follow @ellevest

EngineerGirl
www.engineergirl.org
Follow @EngineerGirlNAE

espnW
www.espn.com/espnw/
Follow @espnw

Female Athletes Rock
www.femaleathletesrock.org
Follow @femaleathletesrock

Frugal Feminista
www.thefrugalfeminista.com
Follow @frugalfeminista

Geena Davis Institute
https://seejane.org
Follow @gdigm #seeitbeit

Girl Scouts
www.girlscouts.org
Follow @girlscouts

Girls Above Society
www.girlsabovesociety.org
Follow @girlsabovesociety

Girls in Politics
www.girlsinpolitics.org
Follow @girlsinpolitics

Girls on the Run
www.girlsontherun.org
Follow @girlsontheruninternational

Girls Who Code
https://girlswhocode.com
Follow @girlswhocode

Girls with Impact
https://girlswithimpact.com
Follow @girlswithimpact

Girls Write Now
www.girlswritenow.org
Follow @girlswritenow

GirlSpire
http://projgirlspire.com
Follow @projectgirlspire

GirlStart
https://girlstart.org
Follow @iheartgirlstart

GoldieBlox
www.goldieblox.com
Follow @goldieblox

iCivics
www.icivics.org
Follow @icivicsinc

If/Then
www.ifthenshecan.org
Follow @ifthenshecan

Ignite
www.ignitenational.org
Follow @IGNITE_National

inLieu
https://inlieu.com
Follow @giveinlieu

Khan Academy
www.khanacademy.org
Follow @khanacademy

Lean In
https://leanin.org
Follow @leaninorg

Mogul
https://onmogul.com
Follow @onmogul

National Coalition of Girls' Schools
www.ncgs.org
Follow @girlsschools

Rock The Street, Wall Street
https://rockthestreetwallstreet.com
Follow @girlsrockwallstreet

Run for Something
https://runforsomething.net
Follow @runforsomethingnow

Running Start
https://runningstart.org
Follow @runningstart

She Should Run
www.sheshouldrun.org
Follow @sheshouldrun

She Started It
www.shestarteditfilm.com
Follow @shestarteditfilm

Smore Magazine
www.smoremagazine.com
Follow @smoremagazine (Twitter)

Stemettes
https://stemettes.org
Follow @stemettes

TechGirlz
www.techgirlz.org
Follow @techgirlz

Teen Ink
www.teenink.com
Follow @teen.ink

The Children's Place
www.childrensplace.com/us/home
Follow @childrensplace

The Mars Generation
www.themarsgeneration.org
Follow @themarsgeneration

The Sparkle Effect
www.thesparkleeffect.org
Follow @sparkleeffect

Tools and Tiaras
www.toolsandtiaras.org
Follow @tools_n_tiaras

Try Engineering
https://tryengineering.org
Follow @TryEngineering (Twitter)

ÊXTRAS

We know we threw a lot at you. And you need details. *We hear you.* Explore each section below for all the links, data points, and original articles on which this book was based. Because . . . smart girls always want to dig deeper.

#BeSmart

"Girls Should Raise Their Hands Instead of Lowering Their Standards," by Illana Raia, Huffington Post, September 12, 2016: www.huffpost.com/entry /back-to-school-five-reaso_b_11982236

"Spoiler Alert: The Nerdy Girl Becomes the Cool Girl . . . Just Watch," by Illana Raia, Huffington Post, February 16, 2017: www.huffpost.com/entry /spoiler-alert-the-nerdy-girl-becomes-the-cool -girl_b_58a61002e4b0fa149f9ac364

Hidden Figures: www.foxmovies.com/movies /hidden-figures

Queen of Katwe: https://movies.disney.com/queen-of -katwe

The Other Einstein, by Marie Benedict, SourceBooks Landmark, 2016: www.authormariebenedict.com

Geek Girl Rising, by Heather Cabot and Samantha Walravens, St. Martin's Griffin 2017: https:// geekgirlrising.com

Girls Who Code (series), by Reshma Saujani, Penguin Random House, 2017: https://girlswhocode.com /books

Mythbusters Jr: www.sciencechannel.com/tv-shows /mythbusters-jr/

"Winner of the Discovery Education 3M Young Scientist Challenge," by Mike Bryant, Discovery Education Blog, November 1, 2016: http://blog .discoveryeducation.com/blog/2016/11/01/winner -of-the-discovery-education-3m-young-scientist -challenge

"Fighting Drought with Fruit," Google Science Fair, 2016: www.googlesciencefair.com/past-projects /deb654bce83b15eed364f52fa8685634649014 602eca78858c58fec00aa6041a

Interview with Emily Calandrelli, conducted October 11, 2017: www.etregirls.com/be-smart.html

"How a Challenge and a Girl Can Change the World," by Illana Raia, Thrive Global, February 12, 2018: https://thriveglobal.com/stories/how-a -challenge-and-a-girl-can-change-the-world

Interview with Gitanjali Rao, conducted January 5, 2018: www.etregirls.com/be-innovative.html

"Why Girls Should Engineer Their Future," by Illana Raia, Huffington Post, August 17, 2017: www .huffpost.com/entry/why-girls-should-engineer -their-future_b_5990a3dfe4b063e2ae0580c0

Dream Big: www.dreambigfilm.com

Underwater Dreams: www.underwaterdreamsfilm .com

Interview with Morgan DiCarlo, conducted July 15, 2018: www.etregirls.com/be-smart.html

"What Is Shine Theory?" by Aminatou Sow and Ann Friedman: www.shinetheory.com

Interview with the STEAM Squad, conducted August 29, 2018: www.etregirls.com/be-smart.html

#BeInnovative

"Five Reasons Why Girls Make Great Founders," by Illana Raia, Huffington Post, October 27, 2017: www.huffpost.com/entry/five-reasons-why -girls-make-great-founders_b_59f21589e4b06 acda25f483a

"Leadership: What Admissions Officers Really Want to See," by Ishan Puri, Huffington Post, September 8, 2016: www.huffpost.com/entry /leadership-what-admission_b_11914438

"For Every Entrepreneurial Girl with a Cool Startup Idea . . . Don't Give Up," by Illana Raia, Huffington Post, April 19, 2017: www.huffpost .com/entry/for-every-entrepreneurial-girl-with -a-cool-startup_b_58f7c438e4b071c2617f0214

"This Awesome Eleven-Year-Old Girl Designed a Prosthetic Arm That Shoots Glitter," by Caroline Bologna, Huffington Post, February 22, 2017: www.huffpost.com/entry/this-awesome-11-year -old-girl-designed-a-prosthetic-arm-that-shoots -glitter_n_58ac8bcce4b0e784faa21a45

"Energy Scooter," Shakeena Julio and Allieberry Pitter, Maker Faire, 2015: https://makerfaire .com/maker/entry/52067

"Thirteen-Year-Old Founder Mercer Henderson Is Creating Apps to Make a Difference," by Tori Utley, Forbes, October 31, 2016: www.forbes .com/sites/toriutley/2016/10/31/13-year-old -founder-mercer-henderson-is-creating -apps-to-make-a-difference/#4dec30bf2c9c

Interview with Jordan Reeves, conducted July 18, 2018: www.etregirls.com/be-innovative.html

Born Just Right: www.bornjustright.org

Interview with Sammy Wolfe, conducted September 3, 2017: www.etregirls.com/be-innovative.html

Information on Club Être: www.etregirls.com /club-ecirctre.html

#BeWi$e

"Financial Confidence in Girls Isn't Impolite . . . It's Essential," by Illana Raia, Huffington Post December 12, 2016: www.huffpost.com/entry /financial-confidence-in-g_b_13573408

"2018 Survey of the States: Economic and Personal Finance Education in Our Nation's Schools," Council For Economic Education, 2018: www .councilforeconed.org/policy-and-advocacy /survey-of-the-states/

Ellevest Magazine: www.ellevest.com/magazine

"Money Matters," Girl Scouts: www.girlscouts.org/en
/raising-girls/leadership/money.html

"Why Explaining Equal Pay EARLY Empowers Girls,"
by Illana Raia, Medium, April 10, 2018; reprinted
on Ellevate Network: www.ellevatenetwork.com
/articles/9186-why-explaining-equal-pay-early
-empowers-girls

"The State of the Gender Pay Gap 2019": www
.payscale.com/data/gender-pay-gap

Equal Pay Day: www.equalpaytoday.org/equalpaydays

"The Gender Pay Gap by the Numbers": https://leanin
.org/equal-pay-data-about-the-gender-pay-gap

"Six Charts That Show the Glaring Gap Between
Men and Women's Salaries," by Sonam Sheth,
Shayanne Gal, and Andy Kiersz, *Business Insider,*
republished April 2, 2019: www.businessinsider
.com/gender-wage-pay-gap-charts-2017-3#the
-number-of-women-promoted-to-the-highest
-levels-of-companies-reveals-unconscious
-biases-6

"The Wage Gap Is Real," Ellevate Network,
April 5, 2018: www.instagram.com/p
/BhMcxCSH2S9/?taken-by=ellevate_ntwk

"A Stunning Chart Shows the True Cause of the
Gender Wage Gap," by Sarah Kliff, Vox, February
19, 2018: www.vox.com/2018/2/19/17018380
/gender-wage-gap-childcare-penalty

"Six Excuses for the Gender Pay Gap You Can Stop
Using," by Alicia Adamczyk, *Money,* April 12,
2016: http://money.com/money/4285843
/gender-pay-gap-excuses-wrong

"Pay Transparency and Equal Pay Protections,"
Women's Bureau, US Department of Labor:
www.dol.gov/wb/EqualPay/equalpay_txt.htm

"America's Women and the Wage Gap," National
Partnership for Women and Families, May 2019:
www.nationalpartnership.org/our-work
/resources/workplace/fair-pay/americas-women
-and-the-wage-gap.pdf

"Ellen Pompeo's Money Advice Will Help You Get the
Paycheck You Deserve," by Olivia Bahou, *InStyle,*
updated March 29, 2019: www.instyle.com/news
/ellen-pompeo-equal-pay-day-negotiate-raise

"Why I'm Fighting for Equal Pay," by Carli Lloyd,
New York Times, April 10, 2016: www.nytimes
.com/2016/04/11/sports/soccer/carli-lloyd-why
-im-fighting-for-equal-pay.html?_r=0

"Abby Wambach on Mission to Empower Women," by
Aimee Lewis, CNN, January 16, 2019: www.cnn
.com/2019/01/16/football/abby-wambach-us
-soccer-equality-spt-intl/index.html

"What Is Equal Pay?" Ellevate, 2019: www
.ellevatenetwork.com/articles/9170-what-is
-equal-pay

"Pay It Forward for Equal Pay Day," Ellevest, March
28, 2019: www.ellevest.com/magazine/disrupt
-money/equal-pay-day

Women. Fast Forward: www.ey.com/en_gl
/women-fast-forward

Own Your Worth: www.ubs.com/microsites
/client-segments/en/own-your-worth.html

"Why Women (and Girls) Should Care About
Crypto," by Illana Raia, Medium, March 29, 2018:
https://medium.com/@illanaraia/why-women
-and-girls-should-care-about-crypto-109db75314

"A Look at Who Owns Bitcoin (Young Men) and Why
(Lack of Trust)," by Kailey Leinz, *Bloomberg,*
January 24, 2018: www.bloomberg.com/news
/articles/2018-01-24/a-look-at-who-owns-bitcoin
-young-men-and-why-lack-of-trust

"Women in Cryptocurrencies Push Back Against
'Blockchain Bros'," by Nellie Bowles, *New York
Times,* February 25, 2018: www.nytimes.com/2018
/02/25/business/cryptocurrency-women-block
chain-bros.html

"'Blockchain Bros' No More: Women in Cryptocurrency Speak Up About Their Accomplishments," by Rachel Wolfson, *Forbes*, March 14, 2018: www.forbes.com/sites /rachelwolfson/2018/03/14/blockchain-bros -no-more-women-in-cryptocurrency-speak -up-about-their-accomplishments /#b79c03349164

"How (and Why) to 50/30/20 Your Money," Ellevest September 25, 2018: www.ellevest.com /magazine/personal-finance/50-30-20-rule

#BeConnected

"Mentors Matter . . . As Early As Middle School," by Illana Raia, Huffington Post, January 11, 2017: www.huffpost.com/entry/mentors-matteras -early-as_b_14093212

Information on Être Lunch & Learn Mentorship Events: www.etregirls.com/be-connected.html

#BeStrong

"Girls, Don't Quit . . . Stay in Your Cleats," by Illana Raia, Huffington Post, May 30, 2017: www .huffpost.com/entry/girls-dont-quitstay-in-your -cleats_b_592ddcdae4b047e77e4c3f31

"Do You Know the Factors Influencing Girls' Participation in Sports?" Women's Sports Foundation, September 9, 2016: www .womenssportsfoundation.org/support-us /do-you-know-the-factors-influencing-girls -participation-in-sports

"Inspirational Quotes from Powerful Feminist Icons," Ellevate Network: www.ellevatenetwork.com /articles/8118-inspirational-quotes-from -powerful-feminists-icons

"Youngest Rio 2016 Olympian Singh Makes a Splash," August 7, 2016: www.olympic.org/news/youngest -rio-2016-olympian-singh-makes-a-splash

"Serena Williams's Pregnant Victory Reminds Us How Amazing Women's Bodies Are," by Natasha Henry, *Guardian,* April 20, 2017: www.theguardian .com/commentisfree/2017/apr/20/serena-williams -pregnant-tennis-women

"When I Play," espnW / ESPN Stories, March 2, 2017: www.youtube.com/watch?v=_eXE1ka4HJs

"#LikeAGirl," Always, June 28, 2016: www.youtube .com/watch?v=Emawq64b0DU

"Modeling the Economic and Health Impact of Increasing Children's Physical Activity in the United States," by Bruce Y. Lee et al., *Health Affairs* 36, no. 5 (May 2017): www.healthaffairs .org/doi/abs/10.1377/hlthaff.2016.1315

"Where Will You Find Your Next Leader?" EY/ESPN, 2015: http://www.espn.com/espnw/w-in-action /2015-summit/article/13844836/how-succeed -business-start-playing-sports-study-says

Interview with Julia Landauer, conducted July 17, 2018: www.etregirls.com/be-strong.html

"Gabby Douglas Joins Anti-Cyberbullying Campaign After Social Media Attacks," by Kelly McKelvey, ABC News, December 16, 2016: https://abcnews .go.com/Entertainment/gabby-douglas-joins -anti-cyberbullying-campaign-social-media /story?id=44218202

"Help Us #HackHarassment," by Cynthia Germanotta, Born This Way Foundation, January 8, 2016: https://bornthisway.foundation/help-us -hack-harassment

Abby Wambach: http://abbywambach.com

"Pakistani Teen Swimmer Blazes Path for Muslim Women," by Craig Lord, *Swimming World,* August 11, 2004: www.swimmingworldmagazine .com/news/pakistani-teen-swimmer-blazes-path -for-muslim-women

"These Four Women from Saudi Arabia Join Olympics, Making History," by Meghan Werft,

Global Citizen, July 29, 2016: www.globalcitizen
.org/en/content/saudi-arabia-women-olympics
-competition

"Billie Jean King," Women's Sports Foundation, June
20, 2011: www.womenssportsfoundation.org
/about-us/people/founder

Interview with Sarah Cronk, conducted February 27,
2019

Interview with Jen Welter, conducted April 9, 2019

#BeInformed

"Be the Girl Who Watches the News . . . But Knows
Her Own Mind," by Illana Raia, Huffington Post,
July 27, 2017: www.huffpost.com/entry/be-the
-girl-who-watches-the-newsbut-knows-her
-own_b_5979e63ee4b06b305561ce55

"Our New Research Shows Where Kids Get Their
News and How They Feel About It," by Michael
Robb, Common Sense Media, March 7, 2017:
www.commonsensemedia.org/blog/our-new
-research-shows-where-kids-get-their-news-and
-how-they-feel-about-it

PBS NewsHour Extra: www.pbs.org/newshour/extra

Smithsonian Tween Tribune: www.tweentribune
.com/category/tween78

TIME for Kids: www.timeforkids.com/g56

NASA's Climate Kids: https://climatekids.nasa.gov
/menu/big-questions

National Geographic Climate Change: www
.nationalgeographic.com/environment
/climate-change

"What Midterm Elections Tell Middle School Girls,"
by Illana Raia, Medium, November 7, 2018:
https://medium.com/@illanaraia/what-midterm
-elections-tell-middle-school-girls-1db6baaef1fb

"2018 Summary of Women Candidates," Rutgers
Center For American Women and Politics,
updated November 14, 2018: https://cawp
.rutgers.edu/potential-candidate-summary
-2018#senate

"Record Number of Women Heading to Congress,"
by Mary Jordan, *Washington Post,* November 8,
2018: https://www.washingtonpost.com/politics
/record-number-of-women-appear-headed-for
-congress/2018/11/06/76a9e60a-e1eb-11e8-8f5f
-a55347f48762_story.html

"Teach Girls Bravery, Not Perfection," by Reshma
Saujani, February 2016: www.ted.com/talks
/reshma_saujani_teach_girls_bravery_not
_perfection?language=en

"Getting Today's Girls on Tomorrow's Ballots," by
Illana Raia, Huffington Post, November 20, 2017:
www.huffpost.com/entry/getting-todays-girls-on
-tomorrows-ballots_b_5a11f3cee4b0e30a
9585084d

Teach a Girl to Lead: http://tag.rutgers.edu

"Women in Elective Office 2019," Rutgers Center for
American Women and Politics, 2019: https://
cawp.rutgers.edu/women-elective-office-2019

"Girls and Leadership," She Should Run / Decision
Analyst, November 4–9, 2016: www
.sheshouldrun.org/girls-and-leadership-research

#BeCharitable

"Be the Girl Who Inspires Giving," by Illana Raia,
Thrive Global, December 23, 2016: https://
thriveglobal.com/stories/be-the-girl-who
-inspires-giving

"Turning the Tide: Inspiring Concern for Others
and the Common Good Through College
Admissions," Making Caring Common Project,
Harvard Graduate School of Education, January
2016: https://mcc.gse.harvard.edu/reports
/turning-the-tide-college-admissions

"Turning the Tide II: How Parents and High Schools Can Cultivate Ethical Character and Reduce Distress in the College Admissions Process," Making Caring Common Project, Harvard Graduate School of Education, March 2019: https://mcc.gse.harvard.edu/reports/turning-the-tide-2-parents-high-schools-college-admissions

Interview with Taylor Richardson, conducted February 20, 2018: https://www.etregirls.com/be-brave.html

Interview with Kathy Terry, conducted March 7, 2019

#BeBrave

Brave Not Perfect, by Reshma Saujani, Penguin Random House, 2018

"Evicting the Obnoxious Roommate in Your Head," by Arianna Huffington, Medium, November 30, 2016: https://medium.com/thrive-global/evicting-the-obnoxious-roommate-in-your-head-1848db7c9d75

"J. K. Rowling's Original 'Harry Potter' Pitch Was Rejected 12 Times," by Randee Dawn, Today.com, October 20, 2017: www.today.com/popculture/j-k-rowling-s-original-harry-potter-pitch-was-rejected-t117763

"Michelle Obama's Advice to Young People in Her New Book *Becoming*," by Frances Bridges, *Forbes*, November 18, 2018: www.forbes.com/sites/francesbridges/2018/11/18/michelle-obamas-message-to-young-people-in-her-new-book-becoming/#75792a646526

"Be Brave Enough to Take a Breath," by Illana Raia, Thrive Global, December 21, 2016: https://thriveglobal.com/stories/be-brave-enough-to-take-a-breath

#BeHappy

"High School Doesn't Have to Be Boring," by Jal Mehta and Sarah Fine, *New York Times*, March 30, 2019: www.nytimes.com/2019/03/30/opinion/sunday/fix-high-school-education.html

Congressional Award: http://congressionalaward.org/about

International Songwriting Competition: https://songwritingcompetition.com

Scholastic Art & Writing Awards: www.artandwriting.org

TED-Ed: https://ed.ted.com

"Playlist: Talks by Brilliant Kids and Teens," *TED Talks*: www.ted.com/playlists/129/ted_under_20

"Associations Between Screen Time and Lower Psychological Well-Being Among Children and Adolescents: Evidence from a Population-Based Study," by Jean M. Twenge and W. Keith Campbell, *Preventive Medicine Reports* 12, December 2018: www.sciencedirect.com/science/article/pii/S2211335518301827?via%3Dihub

"Social Media, Social Life," Common Sense Media, 2018: www.commonsensemedia.org/sites/default/files/uploads/research/2018_cs_socialmediasociallife_fullreport-final-release_2_lowres.pdf

"Pocket. That. Phone." Thrive Global, by Illana Raia, December 22, 2016: https://thriveglobal.com/stories/pocket-that-phone

Photo Creds

All images with text created with Font Candy. Feel free to share from Être's Instagram account (@etregirls). Être is extra grateful to the following photographers for the awesome images used in this book.

SS: Shutterstock; UN: Unsplash; *when there are multiple photos on a page, photographers are listed left to right, and top to bottom.*

Contents, Monkey Business Images/SS; Intro: mavo/SS; Myroslava Malovana/SS; Nejron Photo/SS; Simon Maage/UN; Golubovy/SS; Twinsterphoto/SS; MRProduction/SS; Monkey Business Images/SS; Vagengeim/SS; Monkey Business Images/SS; Jacob Lund/SS; 9nong/SS; 6: Element5 Digital/UN; Syda Productions/SS; Kite_rin/SS; Rawpixel.com/SS; Yulia Grigoryeva/SS; cheapbooks/SS; Monkey Business Images/SS; Rawpixel.com/SS; FabrikaSimf/SS; Brainsil/SS; Oksana Kuzmina/SS; estudioluismatias/SS; 11, John Schnobrich/UN; 13, Adam Miller/UN; 15, Nestor Rizhniak/SS; 20, CGN089/SS; 21, Ian Schneider/UN; 23, GaudiLab/SS; 24, Brocreative/SS; 25, ABO PHOTOGRAPHY/SS; 27, Rawpixel.com/SS; 28: WAYHOME studio/SS; Kseniia Perminova/SS; science photo/SS; GaudiLab/SS; Luis Molinero/SS; Daniel M Ernst/SS; solominviktor/SS; oliveromg/SS; Refat/SS; oliveromg/SS; vasara/SS; Rawpixel.com/SS; 30, HTWE/SS; 31, michaeljung/SS; 37, Prezoom.nl/SS; 39, James A Boardman/SS; 40, Prostock-studio/SS; 42, iordani/SS; 43, Rido/SS; 44: Daniel M Ernst/SS; Vasin Lee/SS; Monkey Business Images/SS; Rawpixel.com/SS; fizkes/SS; Sergey Chayko/SS; Jacob Lund/SS; GaudiLab/SS; Gutesa/SS; 9nong/SS; Jason Stitt/SS; Ryo Yoshitake/UN; 47, PSHere.com; 49, Ellevate Network; 56, André François McKenzie/UN; 59, iko/SS; 60, michaeljung/SS; 61, Andrey Arkusha/SS; 62: Tobias Schenk/SS; Daisy Daisy/SS; Rido/SS; GLRL/SS; Kevin Schmid/UN; Rawpixel.com/SS; michaeljung/SS; karel-noppe/SS; crazystocker/SS; chuckstock/SS; Daniel M Ernst/SS; Elena Elisseeva/SS; 64, Antonio Guillem/SS; 71, michaeljung/SS; 77, gpstudio/SS; 78: marino bocelli/SS; Rawpixel.com/SS; Maridav/SS; Aspen Photo/SS; Form/UN; Dragon Images/SS; Dylan Nolte/UN; wavebreakmedia/SS; Getmilitaryphotos/SS; Monkey Business Images/SS; Lucky Business/SS; J.Robert Williams/SS; 82, Josiah Day/UN; 85, Dean Drobot/SS; 88, Chuttersnap/UN; 93, Selenit/SS; 95, rawf8/SS; 96: Prostock-studio/SS; Rawpixel.com/SS; CONSTANT44/SS; Shift Drive/SS; Priscilla Du Preez/UN; Diego Cervo/SS; Dima Sidelnikov/SS; Antonio Guillem/SS; Dusan Petkovic/SS; DW labs Incorporated/SS; MPH Photos/SS; ALPA PROD/SS; 98, Alena Ozerova/SS; 101, H_Ko/SS; 105, Rohappy/SS; 111, Dusan Petkovic/SS; 112: alexis kapsaskis/SS; Aleshyn_Andrei/SS; Syda Productions/SS; Daniel Clay/UN; Jacob Lund/SS; logoboom/SS; karel-noppe/SS; Kat Yukawa/UN; Rawpixel.com/SS; Daniel M Ernst/SS; golubovystock/SS; Dmytro Zinkevych/SS; 114, everst/SS; 116, John Barry de Nicola/SS; 118, Kan Taengnuanjan/SS; 125, Rido/SS; 126, Jamie Street/UN; 127, Africa Studio/SS; 128: Monkey Business Images/SS; Yulia Grigoryeva/SS; Smolina Marianna/SS; RossHelen/SS; Maksym Fesenko/SS; Smile19/SS; Aleksandr Markin/SS; RossHelen/SS; carballo/SS; Samuel Borges Photography/SS; Joel Mott/UN; Brian Eichhorn/SS; 130, Viacheslav Nikolaenko/SS; 139, Alexandru Zdrobău/UN; 141, sportpoint/SS; 142: AlessandroBiascioli/SS; Dean Drobot/SS; Volodymyr Tverdokhlib/SS; iordani/SS; silverkblackstock/SS; iordani/SS; YAKOBCHUK VIACHESLAV/SS; Katy Anne/UN; Mila Supinskaya Glashchenko/SS; Lopolo/SS; oneinchpunch/SS; Kendra Kamp/UN; 145, Aila Images/SS; 147, lzf/SS; 151, mavo/SS; 152, Cookie Studio/SS; 154, Alena Ozerova/SS; 157, Merla/SS; 158: sianc/SS; Hung Chung Chih/SS; R_Tee/SS; Jason Stitt/SS; PAKULA PIOTR/SS; BestPhotoStudio/SS; Kimrawicz/SS; Monkey Business Images/SS; Gaudilab/SS; Portrait Images Asia By Nonwarit/SS; ollyy/SS; wavebreakmedia/SS; 165, Creativa Images/SS; 167, (UP) vasara/SS; 167, (LO) Marisa Buhr/UN; 168, mangostock/SS; 169, Volodymyr Tverdokhlib/SS; 170, macondo/SS; 171, (UP) Melissa Askew/UN; 171, (LO) Monkey Business Images/SS; 173, My Life Graphic/SS; 175, wavebreakmedia/SS; 177, Leszek Czerwonka/SS; 178, ANURAK PONGPATIMET/SS; 179, szefei/SS; 180, Miguel Bruna/UN; 181, CREATISTA/SS; 188, KIRAYONAK YULIYA/SS; 191, © Erin Borzellino

ACKNOWLEDGMENTS

#TheGirlfriends

Like Heather Terrell, who looked me steadily in the eye and told me I was a true idiot if I didn't build a website for girls. And Heather Shamsai, who knew me in middle school and still offers advice and her daughter's wisdom whenever I ask. Like the sisters-in-law, cousins, Holy Trinity and U of C girls, and the masses of playgroup, book club, neighborhood, and work girlfriends who stand like an army behind every *guess-what-we-should-do* idea I have. I wish every girl out there friends like these.

Être never would have come to be without the following people:

#TheInspiration

When my daughter, Sophia, was in middle school, I realized she wasn't seeing enough female role models. What came next was a series of small lunches that turned into a mentorship project that turned into a website. Yes, you started all of this. No, we're still not getting Être tattoos.

#TheFemaleMentors

Like my mother, the most wildly talented woman I will ever know, who taught me that making a difference is the only thing that matters. And my grandma Spike (yep, Spike), who, as one of the only women in the 1936 class of Brooklyn Law, made me want to study law. Also Nancy Lieberman, the chieftess, at Skadden, for letting me learn at her cuff and for all the feathers. And my mother-in-law, who keeps my eye squarely on the ball.

#THECOOLAUNTS

Don't laugh. There is nothing like an aunt who understands that blue suede clogs can solve a middle school crisis. Or who buys you gorgeous Christmas ornaments because you don't own any. Or who lets you live with her during your first job or shamelessly shares every Facebook post for her niece's passion project. Aunts rule, they just do.

#THEGIRLS

Finally, the girls. Everything good that has come since Être began has happened because of our girls. For our Board of Advisors (100 percent middle and high school girls), who answer monthly emails, give raw feedback, and dream up new people for us to meet, my gratitude. For the girls who join our mentorship visits, start Club Être chapters at their schools, or find innovative ways to mentor local girls, my respect. For the girls we have yet to meet, who pick up this book and think *I so want to be part of this*, everything that comes next is for you.

#THEBOYS

Lest you think that because this book contains only female mentors, my world does too, nothing could be further from the truth. Like my father, who set the bar high and then taught me to clear it. Like Tom Kennedy and Harris Tilevitz, both at Skadden, for creating a role and the job of a lifetime. My father-in-law, uncles, brother, and the cousins and brothers-in-law who are just like brothers. And most of all, for my two Lawrences: my son, for being one of the best writers I know and my arbiter of what's funny; and my husband, who says he doesn't mind being woken up at 5:30 a.m. to decide which Insta post is better, swears he doesn't care that four hundred Être water bottles are owning the hallway, and believes in flowers for no reason. We met in middle school, and I remain the luckiest girl on the planet to be loved by him. Full stop.

EXTRA THX TO

Alexander Rigby, Andrea Kiliany Thatcher, Erin Cusick, Georgie Hockett, Girl Friday Productions, Janet Shapiro, Laura Lee Mattingly, Mike Onorato, Rachel Marek, Sarah Miniaci, and Sharon Thony for brainstorming, editing, and advising with such wise counsel.

"*Être* means 'to be.' I love this word and all the possibilities it evokes. I chose this word for the website I built and now for this book because it echoes my absolute favorite question to ask anyone: 'Who do you want to be?'"

—Illana Raia

Photo © Erin Borzellino

ABOUT THE AUTHOR

LLANA RAIA is a former Skadden lawyer, an occasional guest lecturer at Columbia University, and the founder of Être—a mentorship platform for motivated girls. After an early career in mergers and acquisitions, Illana was named the first Knowledge Strategy Counsel at Skadden, creating internal knowledge sites for more than thirty practices across the globe. She built the Être website with this in mind and thinks of Être as knowledge strategy for girls, curating the resources and role models girls need to change the world. Illana has contributed to the Huffington Post, Medium, Ellevate, and Thrive Global since Être's launch in 2016, breaking down timely topics for the younger set, and was named a Mogul Influencer in 2017. She was featured in The Balance Project Interviews in 2018 and the #WomenWhoRock photo campaign in 2019 and has been a recent guest on podcasts and radio; Illana's journey from attorney to founder was also profiled in *Forbes*. Illana graduated with honors from Smith College and received her JD from the University of Chicago Law School, where she was managing editor of the *Legal Forum*. She lives happily in NYC and at the Jersey Shore with her husband and two children, and is unapologetically nerdy.

CPSIA information can be obtained
at www.ICGtesting.com
Printed in the USA
BVHW020719201019
561565BV00018B/305/P

9 781733 245708